SAP Business Analytics

A Best Practices Guide for Implementing
Business Analytics Using SAP

Sudipa DuttaRoy

Apress®

SAP Business Analytics: A Best Practices Guide for Implementing Business Analytics Using SAP

Sudipa DuttaRoy
Stockholm
Sweden

ISBN-13 (pbk): 978-1-4842-1384-1   ISBN-13 (electronic): 978-1-4842-1383-4
DOI 10.1007/978-1-4842-1383-4

Library of Congress Control Number: 2016959186

Managing Director: Welmoed Spahr
Acquisitions Editor: Celestin Suresh John
Development Editor: Matthew Moodie
Technical Reviewer: Ranjith Raghunathan
Editorial Board: Steve Anglin, Pramila Balen, Louise Corrigan, James DeWolf, Jonathan Gennick, Robert Hutchinson, Celestin Suresh John, Michelle Lowman, James Markham, Susan McDermott, Matthew Moodie, Jeffrey Pepper, Douglas Pundick, Ben Renow-Clarke, Gwenan Spearing
Coordinating Editor: Rita Fernando
Copy Editor: Michael G. Laraque
Compositor: SPi Global
Indexer: SPi Global
Cover image designed by Freepik.com.

Distributed to the book trade worldwide by Springer Science+Business Media New York, 233 Spring Street, 6th Floor, New York, NY 10013. Phone 1-800-SPRINGER, fax (201) 348-4505, e-mail orders-ny@springer-sbm.com, or visit www.springer.com. Apress Media, LLC is a California LLC and the sole member (owner) is Springer Science+Business Media Finance Inc (SSBM Finance Inc). SSBM Finance Inc is a Delaware corporation.

For information on translations, please e-mail rights@apress.com, or visit www.apress.com.

Apress and friends of ED books may be purchased in bulk for academic, corporate, or promotional use. eBook versions and licenses are also available for most titles. For more information, reference our Special Bulk Sales–eBook Licensing web page at www.apress.com/bulk-sales.

Any source code or other supplementary materials referenced by the author in this text is available to readers at www.apress.com. For detailed information about how to locate your book's source code, go to www.apress.com/source-code/.

Printed on acid-free paper

I dedicate this book to my family, for supporting me during the writing and accommodating the irregularities in our life that came along with the time spent on writing. To my parents, my mother-in-law, and my sister, for being there for me. A special dedication to my daughter Anahita, who loves books.

Contents at a Glance

Contents

About the Author

Sudipa DuttaRoy is a Business Analytics specialist with 13-plus years of experience, specializing in SAP BusinessObjects architecture, project leading, business analysis, technical leading, requirement analysis, consumer behaviour analysis and customer segmentation analytics, and providing insights into business processes and strategy, from creating a business case to implementation across several industry domains, such as telecom, retail, insurance, and media.

Sudipa has been involved in projects from end-to-end, starting with initiating business cases, architecture of data warehousing solutions, and platform architecture. Sudipa has held SAP BusinessObjects training sessions and has extensive experience within business intelligence, digital strategies, consumer behaviour analysis, clickstream data analysis, and insight expertise.

Acknowledgments

First, I would like to thank my family for always being there for me, encouraging me, and supporting me. I started working with SAP BusinessObjects about 11 years ago. It has been quite a journey. My first project was about SAP BO reports, from then it has only gotten more and more interesting, with me being involved in every area of SAP Business Analytics.

I would like to thank Ranjith Raghunathan, the technical reviewer, and Matthew Moodie, my editor, for their support and enthusiasm. I would also like to thank Rita Fernando Kim, coordinating editor, for helping to keep things on schedule. She has been an absolute pleasure to work with. I would also like to thank Celestin Suresh John, acquisitions editor, for having spotted me and provided me the opportunity to write this book.

I would also like to thank all my colleagues spread across the globe with whom I have worked over the years. Every project, every complexity has only made me wiser.

Introduction to SAP Business Analytics

Analytics is the driving force in today's business—be it health care, marketing, telecommunications, or retail—and, hence, the most vital part of any organization's strategy. While there are many books that target analytics in parts, this book aims to lay down the end-to-end bits of analytics that any organization can implement.

As the title suggests, the book concentrates on SAP Business Analytics business gains, key features, and implementation. In order for organizations to have a 360-degree view of their myriad technologies and technical solutions, there has to be a strategy in place to converge all the information into one platform. This book explains both the strategy and technical implementation for gathering and analyzing all information pertaining to an organization.

Key features of the book include the following:

- A 360-degree view of an organization's data availability and methods to gather and analyze the same

- Strategies that have to be in place to gather relevant data required from disparate systems

- Details about the SAP Business Analytics suite of products

- Technical implementations to gather data from disparate systems, such as ERP and CRM, and mould the information to gain business insights

- Examples of real-world business cases

- End-to-end technical implementation of the SAP Business Analytics suite of products

- Real-life practical examples of the technical challenges faced

- Examples of different industry domains

The audience for this book includes Analytics strategists, business intelligence (BI) managers, BI architects, business analysts, and BI developers.

The book provides a practically oriented knowledge base for implementing SAP Business Analytics projects, from understanding the business gains of driving BI at an enterprise level to the how-tos of a BI project.

CHAPTER 1

■ ■ ■

Introduction to Business Analytics

Information is advantageous. The more information we have, the better informed our decisions are. We are inundated with information or data in today's world. With about 40% of the world's population using the Internet, and with that number growing every second, data is ubiquitous. We have moved from being an analog world to a very digital one. E-commerce, newspapers, the Internet of things (IoT), music streaming—all generate huge amounts of data. The art of combining every data footprint and gaining actionable insights from that huge cache of data, which helps businesses grow, improves customer experience, and generates revenue, is known as business analytics.

The intelligence generated from data adds value to businesses, by generating leads, retaining customers, increasing revenue generation, gaining competitive advantage, and improving business operations. The data from social media helps businesses understand their customers better. By listening to what their customers have to say about the products and services they offer, businesses can determine if they are losing customers, owing to their competitors' products fulfilling the consumers' needs in a much better way. Market analysis data helps organizations to identify new consumer segments that need to be tapped, unexplored markets, potentially lucrative geographical segments, and spending trends of consumers and consumer-response trends regarding different campaigns. The inventory, web, and other device's log data helps to promote and improve inventory management, data security, fraud detection, IT operations, and online response times, which, in turn, result in better utilization of resources, improved consumer experiences, and innovative business operations. Business analytics is about providing insights, about driving businesses intelligently—and in a fact-driven manner. Previously, data resided in silos, and it was next to impossible to combine sales data with inventory data in an automated way. It required many manual adjustments, resulting in a long, tedious process. But with the advent of business analytics, data integration between different systems is relatively easier and provides a holistic view of an enterprise organization's data.

The process of gathering, combining, exploring, storing, predicting, and utilizing data, and the attendant requirements of a robust IT infrastructure to integrate disparate systems such as order-management systems, ERP, CRM, billing, customer care, market research data, etc., to derive data-driven conclusions, is known as business analytics. Business analytics is paramount for organizations wanting to keep abreast of the digital revolution that has taken the world by storm. Only those organizations that invest in business analytics will lead the pack, as today's consumers demand personalized attention, while, at the same time, their attention span is very short, and there are many competitors vying for the same market.

The different processes that analytics encompass are as follows:

- Data storage
- Data integration
- Data analysis
- Data mining
- Predictive analytics

S. DuttaRoy, *SAP Business Analytics*, DOI 10.1007/978-1-4842-1383-4_1

- Measuring campaign effectiveness

- Measuring online behavior through web analytics

- Data science

- Master data management

- Data security and compliance policies

- IoT

To distinguish the abundance of data from every digital touch point, terms such as *big data* and *data science* were coined. But analytics existed way before big data came into the picture. Earlier business analytics was known as reporting, dashboard, MI (Management Information) reporting, decision support systems, data warehouses, and the like, but it was and is basically data presented in a manner that makes it easy for users to arrive at decisions and predict outcomes. Big data and business analytics are being used synonymously, but analytics can be implemented irrespective of the amount of data. Any business that has the need for improvement—be it in terms of reducing cost, increasing data monetization, enhancing business processes—should start capturing and analyzing data from relevant systems, in other words, turn to business analytics!

The applications of analytics are manifold, not merely to web analytics or financial data analysis. Analytics is being used to save human lives, by analyzing data from wearable devices that measure vital body statistics. This data is also used to further research and development of medicines. Analytics is being used in smart homes, providing centralized control of heating, ventilation, and air conditioning (HVAC) systems. The data from such systems is analyzed to optimize power utilization. In the retail field, data about customer purchase history is being used to send out personalized recommendations to customers. Travel companies thrive on good customer reviews, to attract more customers, and data from social media sites has become very important in gauging customer sentiments about products and services.

With our increased online presence, we leave a lot of digital footprints all over the Internet—when we purchase things, stream movies and music, or participate in online courses or social media. More and more companies have begun analyzing that digital footprint data to gain insights into their business. The more companies know about their customers, the more they can personalize the products and services they offer to their customers. It is not only the data generated by the businesses that is interesting but also that regarding customers' likes and dislikes that can be gathered from social media platforms and business partner sites.

But because analytics is about data, data security and protection laws should be abided by. In short, analytics is a mélange of several processes like the ones named. Analytics requires integrating several systems to enable a holistic view of customer life cycle. Analytics requires data storage management, data security compliance systems, predictive modeling functionalities, and neat and interactive data visualization abilities.

Implications of Business Analytics

Business analytics provides fact-based actionable insights about business data. Fact-based because the data is real, collected from the business processes, and customer interactions. Common examples of data-driven insights are

- Demographics of customers, by segmentation

- Popularity of products bought by customers, by analyzing sales data

- Inventory management, by querying inventory systems

- Online behavior, by analyzing web analytics data

- Targeting of customers for revenue generation, based on their purchase history, by analyzing historical sales data

- Product recommendation to customers, based on their previous online behavior, by using predictive analytics

In order to be able to gain the above insights, many technical systems have to be integrated for data mining. Data analysis requires data from order management to web analytics to CMS (Content Management System) data, some of it being required to be analyzed in real time. Business analytics implementations not only generate revenue and let organizations know their customer needs better but also require that organizations have clear strategies, appropriate IT systems that are easy to integrate, and control over their products and processes. Defining business rules, processes, and products at an enterprise level that can be used as reference data is known as master data management, thereby avoiding confusion. Many organizations that have a global presence use different nomenclature for the same processes and products. Implementing both a local and a global definition for terms and mapping them to each other is a good practice.

For example, in an enterprise organization, payment methods can have both global and local definitions. At a global level, payment methods might be broadly classified as

- Web payment

- Mobile payment

- Credit card

- Bank transfer

- Phone pay

- SMS (Short Message Service)

- Company agreement

- Web payment platform

But local definitions could be country-specific, such as in the case of Swish, a payment method used exclusively in Sweden. But it could be mapped to a bank transfer. Maintaining the data at both global and local levels allows flexibility and analysis of data at different levels. If, for example, a business requirement is to follow up on the total number of bank transfers globally, this also can be achieved locally. For example, the number of bank transfers using Swish in Sweden can be also analyzed globally. Business analytics, although an IT process, is mainly for the business side, so it should be an area of shared competence between IT and business, with typical teams consisting of data architects, data scientists, business intelligence developers, and business analysts who liaise with marketing and sales teams and business controllers or with chief digital officers and other management staff, based on the business case.

Most organizations, even today, have separate business analytics and business divisions, which communicate to each other only when the need arises for a business requirement that transcends both business and IT. Traditionally, business analysts have analyzed functional requirements to translate these to technical specifications, while data analysts are more technical, gathering, cleansing, and analyzing data. To increase the analytics throughput of a company, it is vital to combine the business and analytics competencies, to be able to analyze the data from a business perspective, so as to draw conclusions about consumer behavior, find trends, and, accordingly, implement business decisions with targeted marketing campaigns. It is, therefore, good to have business analysts in the marketing and sales divisions, or to train sales and marketing managers in analytics, so that they are able to analyze data themselves. There are many self-service business analytics tools available that require little or no IT intervention and allow nontechnical business users to analyze and slice and dice data in order to gather insights.

Successful businesses are the ones that consistently achieve their KPIs (key performance indicators). KPIs are a way of measuring results for a business, by analyzing the main business drivers. The main business drivers are not only revenue-generation channels but also business process optimization, cost reduction, optimal resource utilization, and an effective product management life cycle.

KPIs can be defined by

- Pre-defined business processes, revenue margins, and product life cycle milestones

- Strategic business process optimization, cost effectiveness, and product launches guided by quantitative measurement methods

- Analyzing and comparing the achieved goals and revenue against the set goals

Having the right business analytics strategy, based on business goals, is of significant importance. Once the business goals and KPIs are clearly defined, a business analytics strategy can be put in place, suited to the business requirements and the need for data analysis. Every organization has unique requirements and, therefore, its analytics strategy, which takes into account data storage methodologies, the means of data access—such as APIs (Application Programming Interface) or ETL (extraction, transformation, and load), data-visualization tools, and latency and data redundancy to handle exceptions and load balancing, has to be designed according to the business requirements of the organization.

Challenges Faced

Owing to business analytics being able to generate quantifiable facts that provide organizations with a foundation for informed decision making, it is not too much trouble to gain buy-ins from stakeholders or senior management for a business analytics business case. If stakeholders are presented with an analytics blueprint that ensures a return on investment (ROI) that results in a considerable business gain, the stakeholders should be willing to invest in the business case. The challenges, however, arise when the actual implementation of an analytics strategy takes place without prior clear roadmaps having been defined.

Some of the challenges faced in business analytics are as follows:

- *Data integration and too many source systems*: Deriving conclusions that cross over different technological platforms can be challenging. It is advantageous, then, to choose source systems that can be easily integrated into each other and the analytics platform.

- *Data quality issues*: Owing to different source systems maintaining data in different formats, often there are data-quality issues when integrating data from different sources. While it is difficult, organizations should strive to have more standardized data in source systems.

- *Data storage due to huge amounts of data*: With the ever-increasing amount of data, storage becomes an issue. With so many data-storage options available today—cloud, on-premise, appliances and distributed file systems—organizations should choose storage systems taking into account their business requirements and how rapidly their data increases. In some industries such as media, in which it is important to track every mouse click to analyze the traffic, the amount of data that needs to be stored to generate insights is huge. There needs to be a mechanism to handle the storage of data—some operational, some real-time.

- *Response time for data querying*: Querying data may lead to latency, if the amount of data being retrieved is substantial and complex.

- *Long implementation time periods*: Business analytics projects may have long implementation durations, depending on all the aforementioned factors, thereby misleading the stakeholders in their belief that business analytics yields faster results. Iterative processes that deliver value in stages is the right approach.

- *Lack of data governance and metadata management*: This is a very common problem in organizations, as the business sides are not very aware of technical complications that arise due to lack of routines, business definitions, and data-access rights. IT departments can implement the business requirements, but the requirements and definitions have to be defined by the business. Any organization has a defined set of business rules and entities defined by the business, but definitions may vary if there are too many departments involved, or if there are many teams spread out geographically. It is imperative to define business entities and rules at an enterprise level and communicate the same to all departments involved.

- *Lack of knowledge and poor communication between business and IT*: While IT can certainly come up with technical solutions, the business requirements are handled by the stakeholders, taking into account organizational needs. But this could result in a tug-of-war between IT and business, if the responsibilities are not made clear. It is critical that business and IT have a high-level understanding of business alignment and the dependency on each other.

- *No clear strategy in place, hence no clarity on KPIs that drive business*: If there are no clear KPIs defined, it is a hindrance to analytics implementations, as that implies no clarity regarding quantifying goals. If it is not clear what needs to be measured, then the analytics project goals cannot be defined.

While the technical issues can be solved to a large extent as data storage gets cheaper and innovative business analytics tools make data integration easier and cut short implementation durations, it is of utmost importance that data strategies and KPIs that define business goals be in place before any analytics initiative is undertaken. The C-level executives may have in mind a different set of KPIs that drive the overall business, while the middle management may be interested in KPIs that give them insights about efficiency of certain business operations. It is critical, therefore, that the analytics implementation takes into account the expectations of every team that expects a result and that it delivers accordingly.

Conclusion

Business analytics is a multidisciplinary investment, transcending IT and various business departments and involving everyone from top management to the developers who deliver the solutions, thereby creating an atmosphere that encourages knowledge exchange, cooperation, and data-driven processes. This coordination is a side effect of analytics initiatives found across organizations. Measuring, optimizing, and analyzing the effects is what analytics is all about, but, to generate value, it entails overcoming lots of business as well as technical complexities. But when the data chain does deliver great business insights and value, it becomes worth the challenge. The advantages of analytics implementations far outweigh the challenges.

CHAPTER 2

■ ■ ■

SAP Business Analytics Suite of Products

The last chapter discussed the emerging market for business analytics, with data being used to gain insights into every aspect of businesses, and its growing importance in organizations. Businesses that take advantage of business analytics capabilities have an edge with regard to business process optimization and revenue generation.

With the importance of extracting, integrating, storing, and analyzing data for business advancement being at an all-time high, owing to every other organization turning to data for actionable insights, there is a huge market for analytics products. There are myriad solutions available in the market that suit the different needs of gathering, storing, analyzing, and visualizing data. The crux, however, lies in finding the right fit for the job. The key features to looking for the right business analytics product for any given organization are as follows:

- *Ease of integration with other sources*: Do not forget the legacy systems that have to be integrated. The different versions of software updates required, and the need to have other software and operating systems updated to be in sync with them, make certain products cumbersome. If a product requires frequent updating, it is probably unstable, and the maintenance cost may often outweigh the benefit of some flashy features that it may possess.

- *Features and functions that suit the requirements of the organization in question*: A business analytics product could have the best-in-breed features but may lack some particular features that the organization in question requires. In that case, it does not fulfill the business needs.

- *Is, preferably, full stack*: Because an analytics solution requires several layers of product stacks, such as databases, ETL, and reporting and dashboarding tools, having a full-stack solution would mean having the same software vendor's products for each of the layers. This certainly makes it easier to have different modules of the same product suite, as this eases the integrations between different products, making licensing easier and probably cheaper.

- *Promotes self-service*: Business requirement implementations entail IT support and resources for implementation. Empowering business users with self-service products increases organizational effectiveness by reducing the time spent going through several business processes to implement new requirements. In order to implement self-service, the data access and the technicalities involved must be simplified to an extent that allows nontechnical business users to work with minimum technical dependency.

S. DuttaRoy, *SAP Business Analytics*, DOI 10.1007/978-1-4842-1383-4_2

- *Is mobile*: With ever-increasing mobile usage, the need of the hour is to have business analytics products that are mobile-adapted. To be able to access data anywhere, anytime, online or offline, is essential for business users, for effective and quick decision making.

- *Takes a shorter time to market*: Business requirements change quickly and, therefore, require tools and processes that yield results fast. If the implementation time for a business analytics tool is too long, the business requirements may become obsolete by the time the implementation phase is completed. In a world of highly demanding business requirements, a business analytics tool that has a short implementation time is key to serving an organization's analytics needs.

- *Has a reasonable licensing cost*: While choosing an analytics product, licensing costs are an important factor to consider. Usually, product vendors have different pricing models, each having pros and cons. Organizations should weigh these pros and cons and decide which licensing model suits their requirements best, based on the number of server installations, the number of developer licenses, and the number of end-user licenses required.

- *Offers scalability and flexibility*: A product that is scalable is one that is able to handle huge amounts of data, add more users, migrate existing systems, and has backward compatibility. The amount of data that is gathered in today's businesses is enormous and ever-increasing; therefore, the analytics tool chosen should be able to scale the high demands of high-performance organizations.

That said, SAP Business Analytics has a full suite of products covering every aspect of analytics, from data integration to storage, analyzing data in real time, predicting patterns, and visualization. The need to store and analyze data arises from the need to make information available at all levels within an organization, providing easy access, which is a unique selling point (USP) of SAP Business Analytics' suite of products. SAP Business Analytics is meant for enterprise organizations with large-scale information distribution. SAP Business Analytics has such data extraction tools as BusinessObjects Data Services and storage in in-memory databases such as HANA, and includes a number of products for visualization, such as

- SAP BusinessObjects Business Intelligence
- SAP BusinessObjects Dashboards
- SAP BusinessObjects Design Studio
- SAP BusinessObjects Lumira
- SAP BusinessObjects Explorer
- SAP BusinessObjects Crystal Reports
- SAP BusinessObjects Analysis
- SAP Predictive Analytics

Capabilities of SAP Analytics

The capabilities of SAP Business Analytics are manifold, but mainly it distributes data within organizations at all levels, irrespective of the size of the organization, promoting faster time to market and ease of use. SAP Business Analytics shields the business side from behind-the-scene technical complexities involved in integrating, storing, and analyzing data, making it easier for a business to focus on effective decision making.

Some key capabilities of SAP Business Analytics are

- *Improved business user autonomy*: Business users are empowered by being able to access data with greater ease and by faster, mostly by drag-and-drop, functions.

- *Better data governance abilities*: SAP Analytics products have data-level and user-level access rights management in place to implement robust data governance.

- *Faster time to market*: SAP Analytics products are quicker to implement, as SAP understands that businesses are very demanding, and if solutions have a very long implementation cycle, they become obsolete.

- *Integration with existing IT infrastructure*: SAP Analytics has many plug-ins available to integrate with both SAP and non-SAP third-party products. The analytics visualization is compatible with databases such as Oracle, SQL Server, and Sybase or connected to HANA or Hadoop. Organizations that plan to implement SAP Analytics do not have to change data storage in order to be SAP Analytics friendly.

- *Multichannel access to data*: SAP Analytics Mobile solutions enables business users to access data anywhere, anytime, on the go, both online and offline. SAP Analytics Dashboards presents powerful visualizations, including charts and graphs for to enable dashboard consumers to check trends on desktops as well as mobile devices.

SAP Analytics can be deployed in the cloud or on-premises or on a hybrid of both, according to the needs of the organization, thus allowing businesses to focus on their core business, instead of IT infrastructure. The cloud solutions provided by SAP follow the data security and worldwide compliance policies, which, again, offers an advantage to organizations.

Choosing the right analytics tool is not only about being able to create reports and dashboards. If the implementation and delivery of analytics projects go smoothly, delivering results early on, the relationship between business and IT is improved. SAP Analytics provides the kind of agility that business users are looking for: to analyze business data in real time, draw conclusions, take action, and check the response to changes made.

Introduction to SAP Analytics Tools and the Key Features of Each Tool

In a world where business requirements are changing rapidly to accommodate growth—competing with start-ups with shorter time-to-market, launching new products faster to have the first mover advantage—analytics has to keep pace to match the speed. Every business process or product life cycle requires a feedback loop, to be able to analyze cause and effect and to improve business processes and cost-effectiveness. This feedback loop is enabled by business analytics solutions that make valuable information about businesses available in the form of reports and dashboards.

The success of analytics projects depends on the underlying layer of data called the data warehouse, also known as the OLAP (online analytical processing) layer. The data warehouse is the repository of data fetched from source systems such as CRM, ERP, and sales and marketing systems. Data from OLTP (online transaction processing) systems is fetched through an extraction, transformation, and load process that extracts data from source OLTP systems and cleanses, formats, and saves it in the data warehouse. The data in the data warehouse is then presented in a business user-friendly manner in reports and dashboards. Data warehouses store both new and historical data for comparison and trend-analysis purposes, while transactional databases store only current data.

For example: a bank administers millions of transactions every day, with clients withdrawing and saving money, buying financial services, transferring funds, etc. These daily transactions are stored in operational databases, also known as OLTP. OLTP databases enable quick data retrieval when the data to be retrieved is not too huge.

However, if a bank wishes to do some trend analysis related to its most profitable customers or to determine what kind of customers make the most number of transactions over a period of time, OLTP databases are not able to handle such queries, and, therefore, a data warehouse is required. Data warehouses are sufficiently robust, with fewer joins between tables, and they store historical data, facilitating answers to such queries as those preceding. Data warehouses store not only historical data but also data that is blended from different source systems, both at a very granular level, such as transaction ID, as well as at an aggregated level, such as monthly or yearly turnovers. Having data at a very granular as well as at an aggregated level makes it possible for business users to drill up and down and slice and dice data at different levels.

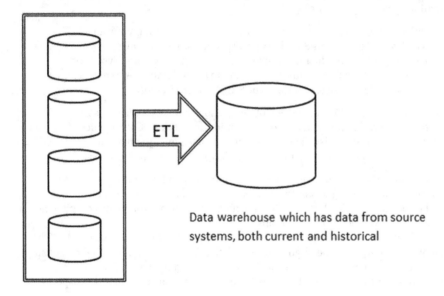

Data warehouse which has data from source systems, both current and historical

OLTP source systems like CRM, ERP, Billing

Figure 2-1. *OLAP databases are sourced from multiple OLTP databases*

Having the strong foundation of a data warehouse enables business users to analyze data in depth. Building a data warehouse depends on a well-designed, scalable data model. SAP HANA Data Warehousing Foundation complements data warehousing capabilities provided by SAP Business Warehouse, SAP HANA Agile Data Marts, and other SAP HANA systems. In order to integrate data from different source systems, cleanse its format, and load it into the data warehouse, SAP Data Services is used as an ETL tool. Once the data has been loaded into the data warehouse, visualization tools, such as SAP WebIntelligence, SAP Design Studio, and SAP Lumira, are used to visualize the data in an interactive manner.

The following sections describe some SAP Business Analytics solutions.

SAP BusinessObjects Business Intelligence Platform

The BusinessObjects Business Intelligence platform is a flexible platform for sharing information within the organization—from CEOs to data scientists to business users. The complexities of the underlying data are shielded by a business user-friendly layer that maps the technical data into corporate business terms. This layer is known as the semantic layer. The semantic layer provides information in a way that is familiar to business users. For example, employee IDs in a database might be saved either as emp_id or empl_id, which is not very clear to a nontechnical user. But renaming emp_id Employee ID in a semantic layer provides business users the relevant data from a business perspective.

Key features of SAP BusinessObjects Business Intelligence platform are as follows:

- *Self-service access to information*: BI developers can publish reports into folders that are directly accessible by business users. Business users have the possibility of creating their own reports, by connecting to the semantic layer, thereby reducing IT dependency and increasing the throughput.

- *Data integration from different sources*: These can be merged into one holistic view to be presented to the end user. Data sources such as ERP and CRM and order-booking systems that have completely different data types and formats can be visualized in a BI platform as the semantic layer handles the complexities.

- *Publishing and scheduling functionality*: These make large-scale distribution possible: BI reports can be shared in different formats, such as Excel or PDF, or can be scheduled, so that users receive them in their mailboxes, or published on portals, for general consumption.

- *Scalability*: Several departments and users in one organization can take advantage of a single platform, making the SAP BusinessObjects BI platform scalable. When the number of users or the number of business areas that require the visualization functionalities of the platform increase or the number of user licenses or added data sources have to be taken into account, the BI platform remains one.

SAP BusinessObjects Dashboards

SAP BusinessObjects Dashboards provides highly interactive and visually rich dashboards. SAP Dashboards provide advanced visualization features such as maps to view geographically distributed data. Color palettes further enhance the aesthetic sense, as do integration options to embed the dashboards into portals.

SAP BusinessObjects Dashboards provides rich visualizations in the form of graphs, bullet charts, pie charts, and scorecards, with such additional features as legends and labels on graphs.

SAP BusinessObjects Dashboards has a thin processing layer between the data sources and the dashboard front end, making data refresh very quick. This is one of the major requirements of businesses: to be able to see business data in real time, in charts and graphs. Easy integration with different data sources and semantic layers highlight the ease that SAP Dashboards provides.

SAP BusinessObjects Design Studio

SAP Business Objects Design Studio enables BI developers to create analysis applications and dashboards based on SAP BW, SAP HANA, and semantic data sources, both for desktop and mobile devices.

End users can create analysis applications using SAP BusinessObjects Design Studio, eliminating the need for BI developers for every new implementation requirement. Design Studio provides drag-and-drop features for easy navigation. With a real-time package available, Design Studio makes it possible to pull real-time data from SAP BW and SAP HANA, to create visualizations in real time.

SAP BusinessObjects Lumira

SAP BusinessObjects Lumira enables users to access, transform, and visualize data in a self-service manner for ad hoc reporting.

The easy interface with drag-and-drop features makes Lumira very user-friendly, even for the least technical business user, eliminating the need for extensive training.

It is truly a low-cost, end user-friendly tool, with easy sharing options, such as publishing Lumira data sets and documents to Lumira cloud, Lumira server, or the SAP BI server. SAP Lumira is mobile-compatible, enabling business users to access data in real time.

SAP Crystal Reports

SAP Crystal Reports provides businesses with pixel-perfect reports for external consumer needs, such as invoices, bank statements, or portfolio letters.

SAP Crystal Reports provides smart default formatting options. It also provides multi-source support and can combine data from disparate sources and present it as one holistic data set.

SAP BusinessObjects Analysis

SAP BusinessObjects Analysis comes in two versions: an edition that integrates Word and Excel for Microsoft Office, and one that is accessed from the BusinessObjects Enterprise BI launchpad in a web browser, which enables users to access data easily, using workbooks.

SAP Predictive Analytics

SAP Predictive Analytics is a statistical analysis and data-mining solution that takes advantage of predictive models to discover hidden insights and trends in data, in order to make certain predictions.

SAP Predictive Analytics combines SAP InfiniteInsight (as Automated Analytics) and SAP Predictive Analysis (as Expert Analytics) to do time series forecasting, outlier detection, trend analysis, classification analysis, segmentation analysis, and affinity analysis.

SAP Predictive Analytics can handle large volumes of data and perform data analysis by using the R statistical analysis language and in-memory data-mining capabilities.

Conclusion

Every business has unique requirements, which keep changing with time and growth. To support business needs, business analytics implementations must always keep abreast of such changes. Therefore, it is important to create a scalable data warehouse, with an ETL design that can easily integrate newer source systems and handle loading of additional amounts of data. The visualization tools chosen should be unique to each business requirement. Some business processes require that analysts analyze the data themselves. In such cases, SAP Business Analysis represents a suitable choice. In other cases, for example, top management may have to check weekly market trends without delving into detail, and that need can be addressed by using SAP Dashboard. Each business must carefully consider its specific requirements before selecting a business analytics tool that fits the bill.

CHAPTER 3

■ ■ ■

Consolidating Data from Disparate Systems for an Analytics Project

Analytics discovers patterns in data, by turning raw data into meaningful information. Analytics implies being able to generate insights by analyzing data generated by business systems. Because every business has several systems that support each business process, it is important that data from these different systems is merged before data analysis begins. This is critical to attaining a holistic view of business processes and the data generated by them. This chapter explains the importance of merging data and its attendant challenges and solutions.

Importance of Merging Data from Different IT Systems

Every organization, irrespective of industry, has several business processes, each supported by several IT products and processes. Each of these IT processes and products yields an insurmountable amount of information, as well as insights, which are of paramount importance for any organization. Businesses have to rely on data to take decisions regarding investments, improving customer relationships, streamlining IT processes, optimizing human resources, etc. Before the invention of computers and state-of-the-art IT processes and products, organizations relied on paper records in order to improve planning. Because data is so important to organizations, a great deal of time and effort is invested in maintaining the quality, relevance, and availability of data.

Organizations typically have transaction processing systems, CRM systems, billing systems, IT networking systems, human resources supporting systems, inventory management systems, and other IT systems that are industry-specific. For example, the health care industry uses systems that monitor heart or pulse rates, and that data is invaluable for research purposes. With the growing needs of an organization, the number of IT systems supporting business processes also increase, each system providing support for specialized business needs. Ever since the Internet came into being, the amount of data has been on the rise, and now, with smart phones and digitalization on the rise, businesses are inundated with data. Often, the data residing in one IT system is different from the other, making integration between systems an uphill task.

A few IT solutions that can be mapped to business processes in any organization, and the integrations required for these solutions to be able to function, are discussed in the following sections of this chapter.

Order Booking Systems

Booking systems are used for creating, managing, and processing orders of any kind, be they related to retail, health care, manufacturing, or telecom. Order booking systems serve as the initial interface between a business and a customer. There are different ways to track business leads and potential markets by using web analytics, but order booking is seen as a confirmation that a lead has been resulted in a customer. Order

© Sudipa DuttaRoy 2016
S. DuttaRoy, *SAP Business Analytics*, DOI 10.1007/978-1-4842-1383-4_3

booking systems have provisions to integrate with other systems, such as ERP, inventory control, billing, invoicing, and CRM. It is crucial for business to know the reason behind the conversion of a lead into a customer. It could be that certain marketing campaigns lead a potential customer to book an order, such as recommending different products on a web site that have caught a customer's eye. While booking an order, front-office representatives are required to check that the product pertaining to the order is available in the inventory, requiring integration with the inventory management system. Once the order is booked, the product has to be shipped, which, again, requires integration with the logistic software solutions. The order booked for a product has to be charged; hence, integration with an invoicing system is crucial.

CRM Systems

These are responsible for an organization's engagement with existing and potential customers, for sales, marketing, and customer service. One of the main success factors that leverages a high ROI on CRM initiatives is to have robust customer master data. CRM relies heavily on customer master data to mail, message, or send out notifications about campaigns. It is thus vital not only to have the demographics of customers updated but also their preferences and interests. Sending out campaigns to customers who are not interested in certain products, or sending out multiple notifications to the wrong customers, can backfire. In order to distribute relevant marketing campaigns for lead generation, the CRM systems not only require integration with the master data but also integration with ERP, to be aware of the product that the customer owns at present, with billing systems to check the customer's invoicing history. It could be a simple business requirement to remind customers about a credit card expiry date. But such a simple requirement gives rise to extracting data from multiple systems, including customer master data, billing, invoicing, and e-mail software systems.

Billing Systems

Billing systems are responsible for collecting consumption data, taking pricing into account, and calculating charges for customers. They are also responsible for processing payments and managing debt collection. In order to calculate an invoice for a customer, a billing system has to check the product or package that the consumer owns currently, the means by which is usually an ERP system or an order booking system. Every organization has a pricing strategy, which could very well be embedded into the billing system or stored in some other software solution. Billing solutions have to delve into the ERP, and the pricing solutions must be able to calculate and invoice the customer. Billing systems are not only used for invoicing but also as a resource for accounting systems involving bookkeeping, budgeting, and forecasting. Several organizations are required to run a credit history check or establish a credit ranking before granting a customer access to their products. This, of course, requires additional integration with external sources for credit evaluation of individuals or businesses that have expressed an interest in becoming potential customers.

Campaign Management Systems

As software solutions to manage marketing campaigns, campaign management systems usually read data from CRM systems, to distribute marketing content to targeted customers. Campaign management software solutions also provide reporting or dashboarding functionalities to measure marketing campaign effectiveness. A campaign management process involves planning, designing, testing, implementing, and execution and analysis of results, which are then useful for optimizing future campaigns. But in order to target the right customers with the right campaigns, integration between customer master data, CRM systems, invoicing systems, and web analytics is almost unavoidable. The most effective campaigns are those that seem tailored to the customer. In order to send out personalized campaigns, businesses are required to do deep-dive into customer information from various systems, to gather as much data about the customer as possible. E-mail software solutions that send out newsletters and other campaigns to customers could backfire and result in customers de-registering from the offered services, if not correctly configured with inputs from IT solutions that support customer life cycle.

Web Analytics

Web analytics encompasses all tools and software solutions used to measure web traffic and online customer behavior, to optimize web usage. Web analytics is used for measuring marketing, sales, UX (user experience), landing page, bounce rates, and market research. It is also used to measure the amount of traffic that originates from social media sites. Again, web analytics products have to be integrated with solutions such as master data or data security solutions to understand the customers that log on to web pages—their usage patterns, fraud detection, and access rights. Web analytics is also used to measure lead generation, and the data resulting from such measurements is forwarded to CRM and campaign management systems, in order to target them better, thus increasing conversion rates for businesses. Capturing clickstream data is a huge challenge for businesses, as a web page could potentially generate millions of clicks in minutes, depending on the content of the page. Furthermore, if there is a business requirement to combine clickstream data with other business data, to generate insights, the solution could encompass several IT systems, making it too complex. But, nevertheless, if it is a must for revenue-generation, data integration between systems has to be achieved in the most optimal way.

Inventory Management

Inventory management systems are one of the most important business systems, because they reflect business investment and the costs incurred before a product is sold. Front-office representatives or salespeople in retail outlets have to rely on the stock available to be able to serve customers better and before making commitments with regard to the availability of any product. Inventory management systems, in turn, have to be integrated with bookkeeping systems, logistics, ERP, and billing. A mismanaged inventory management system can be hazardous to any business; thus, it requires the utmost care and surveillance.

Human Resource Management

Human resource management (HRM) systems administer attendance, payroll, performance appraisals, benefits administration, recruiting, and learning and absence management, to name only a few functions related to personnel. HRM systems are a way to keep track of optimal resource utilization in any organization. Payroll, absence, and attendance are interdependent, and it eases problems if these modules have tight software integration. Payroll and attendance are also used for budgeting and forecasting, requiring an additional integration with those systems. Many organizations not only have built payroll, attendance, absence, performance appraisals, etc., into their HRMs but also recruitment, hiring, employee self-service, and learning management, thus making them quite robust.

Master Data Management

Master data management, as the name suggests, is the administration of the principal source of the most accurate data regarding an enterprise. With innumerable IT systems and tools, data governance is of utmost importance to maintain correct information. In fact, master data management should be considered paramount in any business. Master data management is used to remove duplicates, redundancies, and errors in data. Customer information entered in different systems could have different names or addresses, making it difficult to combine the data from multiple sources. Master data is maintained for products, product codes and hierarchies, partners, suppliers, locations, customer details, transactions, organization hierarchies, etc. Every system, such as billing, ERP, or CRM, should extract the information regarding the preceding from the master data, to retrieve correct and up-to-date information. Not only is the data correct and up-to-date, but if all systems use the master data as a single source of information, then it makes data integration much easier, while reducing redundancy. However, maintaining master data management systems involves a great deal of effort to cleanse, govern, and manage the quality and life cycle of master data.

Mobile Apps

With the rise in the use of smartphones, most companies have invested in building mobile apps that serve customers better while on the go, be they retail companies that send promotional codes and the latest news about their products, banks that allow transactions on mobile apps, travel companies that store all of their customers' travel-related documents in one app for easy accessibility, or media outlets that disseminate the latest news via mobile apps. The app has to retrieve, from transactional systems, data about customer purchase history or customer preferences. The information on the apps about customer interaction is again fed back to response systems, to improve the app features, to come up with better pricing strategies, and to improve and streamline business processes. Moreover, real-time data becomes important for mobile solutions, as customers demand, for example, only the latest news or the latest status related to delivery of their package. This real-time demand for information requires analyzing huge amounts of data that is retrieved from business systems at the same time as analysis is being undertaken. Real-time analysis of data demands that IT systems support data blending in real time, with very little latency. Systems have to handle a variety of data, its volume, and the velocity with which it is delivered.

Business Analytics

Last but not least are business analytics solutions. These incorporate all of the systems and solutions previously discussed and must be able to measure and optimize revenue generation, customer acquisition, and business gain from a holistic point of view. Business analytics can be used as the foundation for decision making, either by humans (e.g., corporate management) or by automated systems (e.g., campaign management systems) that distribute campaign content via e-mail to customers, based on their interests, the data for which having been fed into business analytics from web analytics or CRM. Business analytics is a fact-based science, driving business decisions by gathering, cleansing, and analyzing data from multiple source systems, such as those mentioned previously. It is business analytics systems that gather and store historic data from each of these business support systems, turning raw business data into valuable information that helps businesses support decision making.

For example, in order to examine a customer life cycle, increase customer satisfaction, and win customer loyalty, organizations have to check related data, from the time the customer bought a product or service, his or her invoicing history, past purchase history, membership points, etc. This data resides in multiple IT solutions. Adding to the list of traditional IT systems, there are now also mobile apps and web analytics data that reveals information about customer online behavior, how they browse products on web sites and on mobile apps, what leads to a purchase, and what makes customers abandon shopping carts. So, the variety of data that has to be stored and analyzed is increasing, and so is the amount of both structured data from traditional IT systems and unstructured data from social media platforms.

If data from these multiple systems is not integrated, the business value it generates is minimal. Data in silos, such as illustrated in Figure 3-1, generates very narrow visions of the business. Data duplication, redundancy, and mismatch are some of the results of data residing in silos—a complete nightmare for enterprise organizations.

Data Silos

Figure 3-1. *Data Silos (Source:* `https://tobeggardescription.files.wordpress.com/2012/02/silos.png`*)*

The data in each of these systems contains in-depth information pertaining to the system in question. A billing system can also act as a reporting system to provide information about important billing KPIs, such as the total number of invoices sent, the total number of payments received on time or delayed. Similarly, an ERP system can also provide some basic reporting capabilities, such as the products owned by a certain customer, or which are the most popular products bought by customers. These isolated pockets of information do not offer sufficient insight into the business as a whole. The data residing in each of these silos is invaluable, no doubt, but it does not provide a 360-degree view of a customer or the entire customer life cycle.

Integrating disparate IT systems to gain business insight is, therefore, imperative. It is not an option but a must. A simple query raised by the business, such as finding the product owned and the amount charged to the customer, requires the amalgamation of more than two IT solutions, making it cumbersome, if they are not already integrated.

To be able to function optimally, every IT solution requires integration with several other IT solutions. Following is an example of the integration required by an ERP system, in order to obtain the most from all of its modules for asset management. ERP requires integration with resourcing, to check the inventory for the availability of a product, integration with logistics, for shipping a product, integration with CRM, to ensure delivery and track the customer engagement with a product, and integration with financial management, to track the invoicing of a product to the customer (see Figure 3-2).

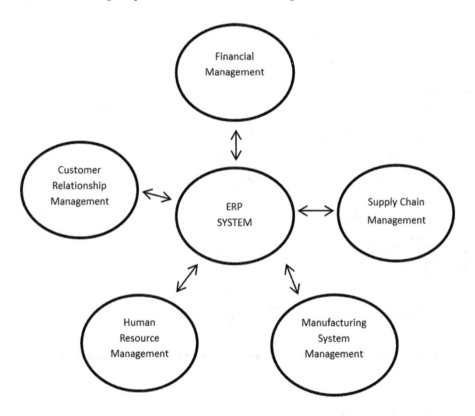

Integrations required for an ERP system

Figure 3-2. *Data integrations required for a typical IT system. The figure diagrams an ERP system. (Source: http://www.newpeaksolutions.com/wp-content/uploads/2015/03/ERP.jpg)*

Challenges Faced During Data Integration

A typical data integration scenario, such as that illustrated in Figure 3-3, is a convergence of multiple sources, including CRM, billing, campaign management, social media, and inventory management, into one single source for analytics. It may appear simple on the surface, but it is quite daunting to integrate different sources of data with different data structures and business rules governing each solution. However, data integration leads to insights for increasing cross-selling and up-selling, by blending data at various levels and from different divisions of a company.

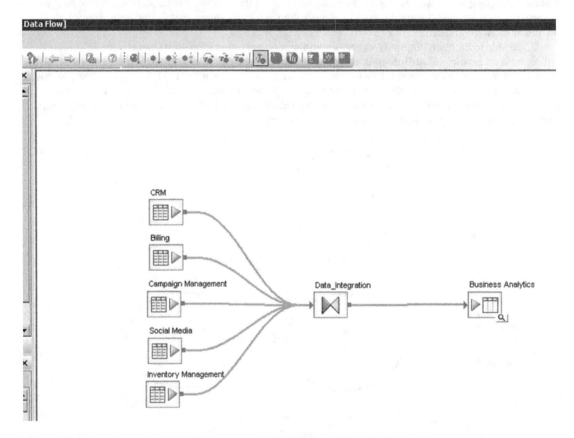

Figure 3-3. *Data integration in an ETL process, in SAP BusinessObjects Data Services*

Some of the main challenges posed by data integration across IT systems and solutions and across data silos follow.

Understanding Business Needs

Taking into account business needs that are the basis for data integration is key. Any organization that focused on a data-integration roadmap must map the business requirements to the business processes and integrate the tools and solutions that support the same. Data integration is a technical challenge, involving time and resources. It is necessary, therefore, to understand the business gain that can be achieved by integrating data from disparate systems, efficiently utilizing time and resources.

Some data integration projects launch even before a business gain has been clearly identified. This leads to the project going haywire and to time and resources not being utilized efficiently. Once business goals are defined, the processes and data required to ensure them are not very tricky to put in place.

The foundation for data integration should be nothing other than a business gain. If the organization is clear about the goals that it intends to achieve by data integration, the process of integrating two or more systems to acquire the added advantage of data blending becomes technically do-able.

Understanding Data-Quality Issues

In a data-integration project, because the sources of data are different and come from different IT solutions, the format and structure of data is not the same. Differing data types, formats, and structures present a big challenge when integrating data from disparate sources. Moreover, some organizations have operations spread out across the globe, introducing the challenge of multilingual text characters. Some software solutions do not support certain languages.

If we consider the example of integrating customer data from a CRM system and a billing system, it is very much possible that some of the data resides in both the systems, giving rise to data duplication. It is then of utmost importance to find out which of the data sets is the correct one and refer it to the master data and map the differing data records into the same.

By focusing on one entity, such as the customer number or the product code, the attributes that lend completeness to the entity in question get easier to understand and easier to map from different systems. For example, customer ID is present in most IT solutions that save customer information as the single unique identity. A customer could have product IDs in ERP systems that point to the products owned by the customer; the customer ID in billing could point to the invoicing address credit card number, and the method of payment that the customer has chosen; and the customer ID in web analytics points to the online preferences and interests the customer has. When gathering data regarding the customer from ERP, billing, and web analytics, there should be one data record that displays the customer's customer ID, billing ID, asset ID, and all the attributes associated with the same—billing address, online preferences, products owned, invoicing method, etc.

If there are cases in which the data contains null values or wrong data, the business has to take ownership of the data that flows into business analytics. Business analytics solutions do not create new data; they cleanse, transform, and modify data to be presented in a way that makes it easy to draw conclusions about customer behavior, product popularity, sales, and marketing.

Data Governance Issues

Data governance is the practice of acquiring, cleansing, and distributing data, accessing rights management, and maintaining security of data. A typical enterprise organization houses numerous departments, each department in turn being run by several software solutions to support business processes (see Figure 3-4). In order to avoid data duplication and redundancy while also maintaining data security, data governance comes into the picture. It is very important to have a master data management system in place that defines the key attributes of the core business.

For example, if an insurance company has 200 products with 50 subproducts under each one of them, this should be clearly defined in a master data store. Every time that a product or a subproduct is referred to or has to be validated, it is this master data source that must be used as the single source for validation or data reconciliation. If this practice is maintained enterprise-wise, not only does it reduce the overhead of maintaining several redundant data stores, but it also eases the distribution and security issues of data.

Data governance also handles access rights to the data. Sales and marketing data, even within the same organization, can be sensitive information, and not everyone should have access to it. Data governance rules clearly define the access levels and rights that different groups or individuals are assigned within an organization.

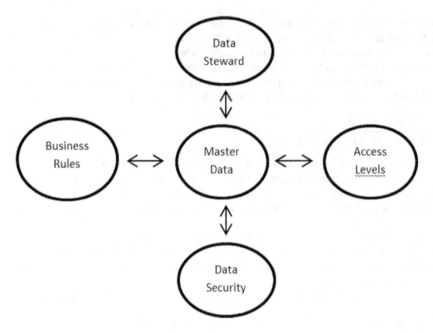

Figure 3-4. *Master data management*

Maintaining Historical Records

Transaction-based systems usually store snapshots of data, lacking historical records. In business analytics, historical data is of utmost importance to check past trends, compare them with prevailing trends, or predict future trends. Transaction processing systems such as order booking have to process huge amounts of data on the fly, the emphasis being on very fast query processing and maintaining data integrity. But if the business requirements are to be able to analyze historical data alongwith fresh real-time data, both have to be integrated, blended, and stored in data warehouses. To save data from multiple sources and spanning different time periods is challenging and requires maintaining data with business rules that were applicable in the past along with data maintained according to updated business rules and, moreover, with differences in structure and format.

For example, combining historical data from a billing system with tariff plans and pricing strategies that were applicable in the past with data from an ERP system with an updated product structure is not only complicated to integrate but will also require a lot of data cleansing and processing, in order for useful insights to be generated.

Storing historical records implies great amounts of data, and that can pose a problem. It becomes necessary, then, to choose the kind of scalable hardware that is able to support growing amounts of data.

Different Data Formats in Different Systems

As discussed, data from different sources generates data in different formats, structures, and size. A customer ID in a billing system could be a character field with a length 100, while the same customer ID could be a numerical field in CRM, thus making integration between the two systems problematic.

An integral component of data integration in business analytics is ETL part (extraction, transformation, and loading). This is the practice of extracting data from source systems, cleaning and processing it in a way that makes it possible to combine data from single or multiple, identical or disparate systems (see Figure 3-5).

In the preceding example of customer ID from two different systems that have different data structures, it is in the ETL process that one of the data types is converted to match the other, to maintain conformity and make data integration possible.

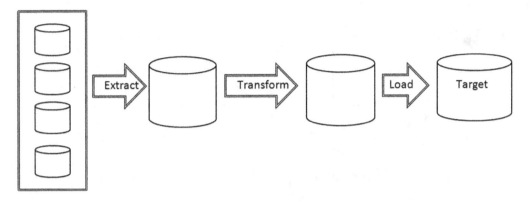

Figure 3-5. *ETL—extraction, transformation, and loading of data*

Data Integration Techniques

To extract data from multiple systems, a data-integration mechanism, such as plug-ins, adapters, and APIs, has to be available. Today, most software solutions are equipped with some form of data connector to integrate with myriad data sources. Data sources being spread over organizations can be on-premise, cloud-based, or remotely situated and have completely different interfaces with which to integrate with multiple systems.

The problem arises with the increasing complexity to connect to each of these connectors. A web service may very well have APIs available but require much tweaking and coding to be able to integrate with another source, demanding additional time and resources. Every day, more and more software solutions are offering ingenious ways of offering multisource connectivity.

Solutions to Combine Different Data Sources

Combining data from multiple heterogeneous systems is an old practice. Comparing Excel sheets stating the cost of marketing campaigns against actual sales has been a longtime standard practice. But with new age digitalization taking the world by storm, and all business systems being supported by software solutions, combining the data from each of the sources is a critical need of contemporary businesses. Combining data from multiple business processes yields an enterprise-wide view of data. Integrating financial data from sales, marketing, supply chains, and human resources empowers many departments in an organization to plan, implement, invest, and optimize their operations much more efficiently, with fact-based figures (see Figure 3-6).

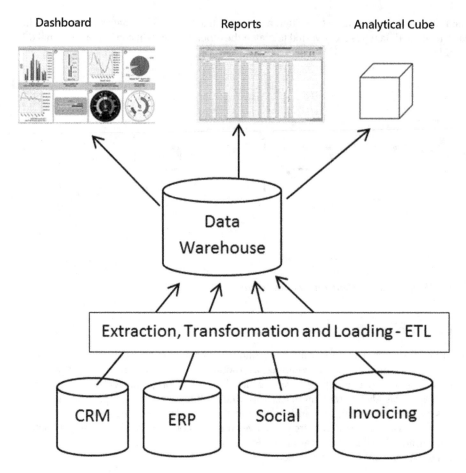

Figure 3-6. *Gathering data from different source systems in a data warehouse that caters to business analytics systems—dashboards, reports, and analytical cubes*

However, integrating multisource heterogeneous data entails a systematic chain of processes to refine data to an extent that it generates information that can be rendered useful by organizations. The following sections elaborate the steps used to process data during a data integration process.

Data Cleansing

Raw data from source systems is as per the standards and rules applicable in the source system, which may not necessarily be the same across all the other systems that have to be integrated. Common fields that have to be handled during this stage are date fields. Dates could be defined in different formats, depending on the source system. Some enterprise organizations have businesses spread across the globe, each country having specific time zones and date formats. Standard business rules that are relevant to all the systems involved must be defined before applying cleaning mechanisms.

For example, an organization may choose to concatenate first names and last names of customers residing in any source system, while combining the sources or adding the country code to all phone numbers.

Removing Duplicates

It is evident that while trying to combine data from multiple sources there is bound to be duplication. Again, predefined business rules determine the method used to eliminate duplicate data records.

Let's consider a customer in a CRM system who has purchased multiple products at different time periods. If the business requirement is to store every record in order to analyze all the products that a customer has purchased during a certain period of time, the multiple records can be considered relevant. However, if the business requirement is to save the record pointing to the latest product acquired by the customer, then all other multiple records are considered as duplicate and must be eliminated. Similarly, if a customer has changed address several times, is it relevant for the business to store all of the customer's previous or only the latest? There could also be scenarios under which the records are identical, such as a data record pertaining to customer details that may have the same information as a data record from web analytics. In such a case, the business would have to determine which record to discard.

Applying Integrated Business Rules

Consider a logistics company that calculates the estimated time of delivery of packages and compares that to the actual time in which packages are delivered. It is the business side that determines how the estimated and actual time required for delivery of packages is derived, which touch points are to be taken into account, and which processes and rules define a delay, etc.

If the business requirement is to integrate all the source systems that contain information regarding geographic locations that the company delivers to, postal tracking systems, scanned data from handheld devices, data quality issues arise, owing to data-redundancy and data-structure differences. Business rules are, therefore, critical to maintaining quality and relevance of data.

Clearly defined business rules, when mapped to software solutions and systems, are easy to maintain and have faster implementation cycles.

Maintaining Master Data Management Systems

The importance of master data management systems cannot be overemphasized. With businesses becoming increasingly diversified, offering innumerable services at the same time and targeting customers of various segments, the increases in complexity become manifold.

To mitigate this growing complexity, it is paramount to maintain master data records of all products on offer and all geographic locations in which customers can avail themselves of those products. In other words, maintaining a single hub, with updated and relevant versions of the key attributes of the business, simplifies business execution and presents a single unified view of enterprise information. Maintaining master data management aids in synchronizing financial and operational strategy and eases distribution of information to a wider audience while reducing costs, by eliminating the overhead associated with maintaining several data silos.

Avoiding Data Silos

Every company is organized in divisions, departments, or groups, such as sales, technology, and finance, that specialize in certain areas. This, of course, results in implementing software solutions that aid the specialized processes required by each distinct division or department. These isolated areas of information are called silos.

Problems arise when the data silos have to be integrated, in order to deliver, across divisions and departments, business insights to facilitate up-selling or cross-selling. Each silo has its own set of business rules, making data integration with other systems problematic. It is, thus, best to avoid data silos in the first place. It helps to take enterprise-wide steps to avoid generating data silos, by having in place an enterprise architecture team that examines new IT investments and integration architecture. Businesses often acquire new tools to solve short-term business goals that otherwise have a long implementation cycle. These short-term solutions gradually turn into permanent data silos. Having an enterprise architecture team that centralizes the IT investment roadmap and software solutions reduces clusters of data silos.

SAP Business Analytics Tool to Combine the Different Data Sources

As a leading business analytics product vendor, SAP has a whole suite of analytics products geared specifically either to large and medium-sized organizations. As discussed, to be able to utilize analytics to the fullest, organizations must integrate data from disparate systems. Raw data from multiple systems makes much more sense when combined to leverage insights. SAP offers SAP BusinessObjects Data Services as a tool for data integration, data quality, and data profiling.

SAP BusinessObjects Data Services (BODS) facilitates extraction, integration, and transformation of raw data from multiple business sources to deliver powerful insights for business gain.

Data and systems management tools that IT departments can use to administer BODS include

- BI platform Central Management Console (CMC)

- Data Services Management Console

- Data Services Server Manager

- Data Services Repository Manager

- License Manager

The preceding list of products will be discussed in detail in Chapter 4.

BODS provides integration support for a number of tools, platforms, and databases, including DB2, MySQL, Oracle, SQL Server, and Teradata; a Universe connection using JDBC or ODBC; and Salesforce integration via Salesforce adapter. BODS also provides integration with big data platforms such as Hadoop.

In order to utilize the data integration and its quality and profiling abilities, to maintain an optimum base for business analytics, clear rules have to be defined with regard to architecture, business rules, cleansing, and transforming, as well as version control of code. Some organizations choose to have most of the data transformation logic in the ETL tools, making it easy to change or upgrade databases without much dependency. But some organizations choose to push querying and data processing to the database level and use ETL as a means of data transfer.

Irrespective of the approach chosen, clear guidelines have to be defined beforehand for

- Data cleansing and transformation

- Understanding data dependencies

- Error handling

- Applicable business rules

- Version control between development, test, and production environments

- Documentation

BODS offers a palette of different transformations that can be used while integrating and transforming data from multiple sources. The following image (Figure 3-7) gives an overview of the functions available for data transformation in BODS, including data transfer, date, hierarchy flattening, etc.

Transform	Usage	Description
⊟ Data Integrator		
Data_Transfer		Allows a data flow to split its processing into two sub data flows and push down resource-consuming operations to the database server.
Date_Generation		Produces a series of dates incremented that you specify.
Effective_Date		Calculates an 'effective-to' value for data that contains an effective date.
Hierarchy_Flattening		Flattens hierarchical data into relational tables and produces a description of the hierarchy in vertically or horizontally flattened format.
History_Preserving		Creates a new row only for each row flagged as UPDATE in the input data set.
Key_Generation		Generates artificial keys in a table starting after the maximum existing key value in the table.
Map_CDC_Operation		Maps CDC data using required input columns.
Pivot		Rotates the values in specified columns to rows.
Reverse_Pivot		Rotates the values in specified rows to columns.
Table_Comparison		Compares two data sets and produces the difference between them as a data set with rows flagged as INSERT, UPDATE or DELETE.
XML_Pipeline		Reads and processes large XML documents in small batches.

Figure 3-7. *Transformation functions available in SAP BusinessObjects Data Services*

There are also a number of data-quality functions available, such as Data_Cleanse, USA_Regulatory_Address_Cleanse, Match, etc. (See Figure 3-8.)

Transform	Usage	Description
⊟ Data Quality		
Associate		Associate Base Transform
Country_ID		Country ID Base Transform
Data_Cleanse		Data Cleanse Base Transform
DSF2_Walk_Sequencer		DSF2 Walk Sequencer Base Transform
Geocoder		Geocoder Base Transform
Global_Address_Cleanse		Global Address Cleanse Base Transform
Global_Suggestion_List		Global Suggestion List Base Transform
Match		Match Base Transform
USA_Regulatory_Address_Cleanse		USA Regulatory Address Cleanse Base Transform
User_Defined		User Defined Base Transform

Figure 3-8. *Data quality functions available in SAP BusinessObjects Data Services*

The BODS architecture, data connectors, and functions are explained in detail in Chapter 4.

Conclusion

You have seen the importance of data integration in business analytics to provide a 360-degree view of business data. Business analytics almost always entails integrating several business systems, to turn data into insightful information that businesses can act upon. However, easy as it may sound, data blending is far from simple. Blending data from different business processes requires cross-platform data retrieval and storage in an enterprise data warehouse that serves as a central repository for all the business analytics requirements of an enterprise.

CHAPTER 4

■ ■ ■

SAP BusinessObjects Data Services

In this chapter, you will discover the advantages of data integration and the challenges faced in integrating data from different systems and in different formats, and some of the proven solutions. The chapter also mentions some common data warehousing practices and technical implementations of ETL (extraction, transformation, and loading).

Introduction to SAP BusinessObjects Data Services

Data from structured sources such as ERP, CRM, and order management systems, when combined with unstructured data from social media and web logs, generates invaluable insights about any business in question. Simple as it may seem, the technical implementation of the same is extremely complex. The technical complexities are not just confined to fetching and blending data from different sources, but they also involve the way data is stored and data-quality issues.

It is a technical challenge to combine different data sources from different technical platforms, because data from different sources have different formats. Data quality also becomes an issue when integrating different data sources. Most of the time in IT departments is spent in trying to integrate multiple data sources rather than in gaining insights by blending data. To manage costs and yet deliver value by tackling complexities is key.

SAP BusinessObjects Data Services addresses the aforementioned challenges of combining data from different business sources while maintaining the quality to deliver information. SAP Data Services fetches data from different business systems and stores it in a data warehouse that is then used to create reports and dashboards to visualize data, thus helping business users with decision making. Different departments in organizations often create data silos that are difficult to integrate with other business data. Apart from complexities that arise owing to data silos, there are complexities such as data duplication, quality issues, and inconsistencies, apart from data types being different. Data Services helps uncover data-quality issues early in the process, by detecting business rule violations in the data flows. Data Services is a single enterprise solution that can be implemented for data integration, data profiling, quality checks, and text processing, facilitating combining data from multiple disparate sources. SAP Data Services eases the process of accessing data from a variety of sources, cleansing and standardizing data in a format that is easily understandable by business users. SAP Data Services provides functionality to analyze lineage to determine data sources of documents and reports. It also provides the functionality to conduct an impact analysis for changes in source or to allow data stores and version-control capabilities to have control over each object over time.

SAP Data Services provides several connectors to access data from various sources through APIs, adapters, and connectors. SAP Data Services can access business data from source systems such as ERP and CRM, and SAP BW or Salesforce, in the form of files using data connectors or adapters to connect to the

© Sudipa DuttaRoy 2016
S. DuttaRoy, *SAP Business Analytics*, DOI 10.1007/978-1-4842-1383-4_4

source systems. SAP Data Services captures data from SAP Netweaver and ABAP. Data Services versions 4.2 onward make it possible to access data from MongoDB and HIVE through adapters and push the data into target data stores.

A Data Services implementation can adapt to an already existing stack of technical tools via web services or APIs. Developers and end users can access, create, edit, and combine data from multiple sources with Data Services projects, using tools such as:

- Designer

- Management Console

- Administrator

- Impact and Lineage Analysis

- Operational Dashboard, displaying the status of scheduled ETL jobs

- Auto Documentation

- Data Validation

- Data Quality Reports

As seen in Figure 4-1, the start page of SAP Data Services displays all the options available in the Data Services Designer. The start page provides a single platform on which to check the repositories, the release notes, SAP community network links, tutorials, etc.

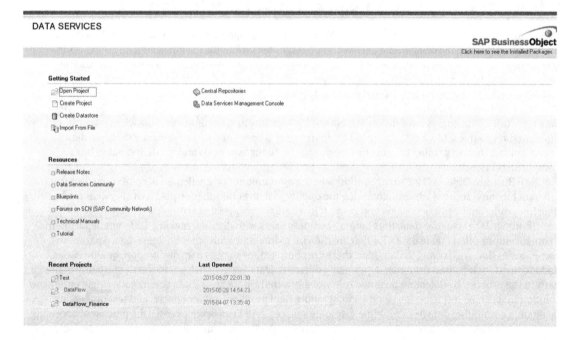

Figure 4-1. *The options provided in the SAP Data Services Designer from the start page*

To manage the data governance for the SAP Data Services set of tools, IT departments can use such integrated tools as the Central Management Console (CMC), Data Services Management Console, Server Manager, and Repository Manager.

Central Management Console (CMC)

The CMC (Figure 4-2) is used for

- Repository configuration
- User administration
- User group administration
- Application rights

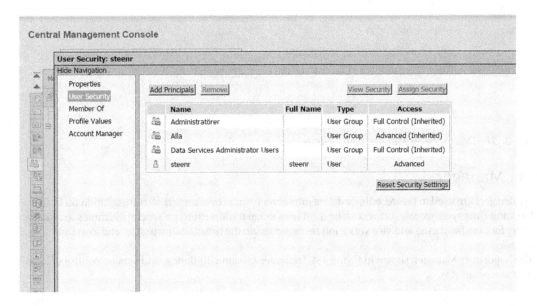

Figure 4-2. *SAP Data Services user management can be handled through the SAP BI platform Central Management Console*

Management Console

Data Services' Management Console can be used to schedule, monitor, and execute batch jobs. Other functions that can be performed using the Management Console are

- User administration
- Configuring and managing adapters, such as Salesforce adapters
- Configuring, starting, and stopping real-time services
- Configuring Job Server and repository usage

In Figure 4-3, the Data Services Management Console start page displays the options available in the SAP Data Services Management Console.

Figure 4-3. *The Data Services Management Console*

Server Manager

Server managers are used to create, edit, or delete job servers and access servers after installation on both Windows and Unix systems. Job servers can be used to manage multiple jobs on several machines to a single repository for load balancing and vice versa. Job servers provide the functionality to start and stop Data Services services.

The Repository Manager, shown in Figure 4-4, facilitates creation, updating, and version control of local and central repositories.

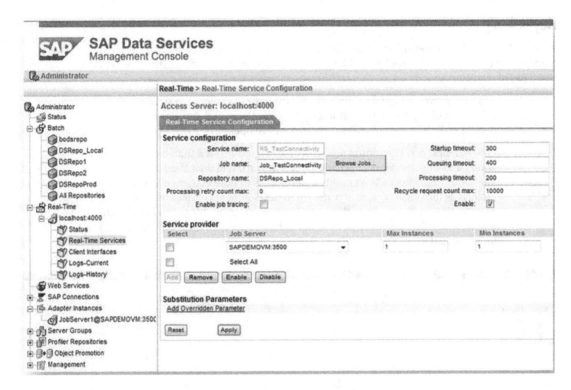

Figure 4-4. *Repository Manager in the SAP Data Services Management Console*

SAP Data Services is accessed and managed through interfaces such as Designer, Repositories, and Job Server. Following is an introduction to each of the interfaces available.

SAP Data Services Designer

Designer is a development tool with a graphical user interface. It provides projects, data mappings, transformations, and source and target configuration options.

In Designer, source data stores such as ERP, CRM, or flat flies from FTP servers, Excel sheets, or database connections such as Microsoft SQL server, Oracle, HIVE, or Mongo DB can be specified with requisite connection information. The data from these source systems can then be accessed, modified, or have business rules applied via Data Services transformations, and validated. Each instance of Designer can be used to connect to the local and the central repositories and also to different environments such as test, development, or production.

Repository

The SAP Data Services repository is the metadata for the source and target data store. Each repository is registered in the CMC and is associated with one or more job servers, which run the jobs created. There are two types of repositories:

1. *Local repository*. A local repository is used by an ETL developer to store definitions of objects such as projects, jobs, work flows, and data flows, developed locally and accessible only to the developer.

2. *Central* repository. The central repository (see Figure 4-5) is a shared object library allowing developers to check objects in and out of their local repositories. The central repository allows multiple developers to store master copies of projects as the single version of truth. Upon development completion, data flows and projects are checked into the central repository, to be able to be shared with a team of ETL developers. Figure 4-5 shows how to access the central repositories from within the SAP Data Services Designer.

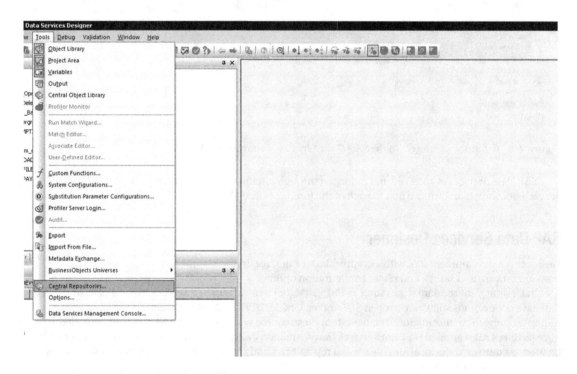

Figure 4-5. *Central repositories from within SAP Data Services Designer*

An SAP Data Services instance can have multiple repositories, such as one for a test and one for a production environment. A single SAP Data Services instance can connect to either. Figure 4-6 shows how to activate one of the repositories. When a developer develops an ETL job in the test environment and, after having tested it, has to promote it to the production environment, the job can be added by a right-click to the production repository, by switching to the right repository.

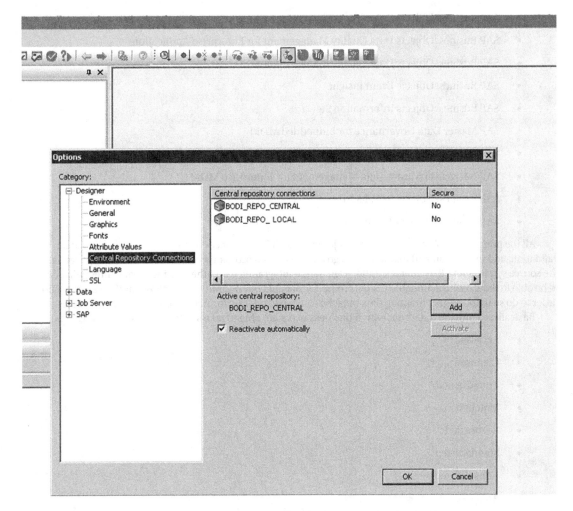

Figure 4-6. *Activating one of the repositories from within the SAP Data Services Designer*

Job Server

The SAP Data Services Job Server is responsible for performing extractions from multiple sources and complex data transformations, loading and integrating numerous systems such as ERP and CRM data, for example. While running a Data Services job, the job server retrieves the job from its repository and starts an engine to process the job. Jobs can either be run locally and in real time in the local repository or run as a batch job, configured in the Management Console. Load balancing can be handled by creating job server groups, which distribute the system load optimally.

SAP Data Services Architecture

The SAP Data Services architecture consists of various tiers of user interface, platforms, and repositories.

SAP offers other products that complement SAP BODS and provide additional SAP BusinessObjects enterprise information management solutions. These include

- SAP BusinessObjects Data Federator

- SAP BusinessObjects Data Quality Management for Enterprise Applications

- SAP BusinessObjects Data Quality Management SDK

- SAP BusinessObjects Event Insight

- SAP BusinessObjects Information Steward

- SAP Master Data Governance for Embedded MDM

- SAP NetWeaver Business Warehouse (BW)

- SAP NetWeaver Master Data Management for Enterprise MDM

- SAP BusinessObjects Rapid Marts

- SAP BusinessObjects Text Analysis

All the preceding tools can be used in conjunction with Data Services to conduct data profiling, data validation, and integration and maintain data governance. Data profiling is the process of verifying that data in the source system looks like what it should, even before integrating with other business data. Integrating data to be able to draw useful actionable insights requires that data be continuously analyzed and measured, and in order to do so in the correct manner, data must be cleansed and transformed according to business rules.

Basically, to provide data from which business users are able to take strategic decisions, it has to be

- Accessed

- Cleansed

- Transformed

- Matched

- Reconciled

- Standardized

- Consolidated

- Analyzed

- Measured

- Optimized

- Automatized

- Improved

To improve data quality and meet business needs is a continuous process, as business requirements often change. To keep up with business needs, data transformation has to follow pace. For example, the business need at one point of time may require accessing and extracting only the data pertaining to order management, but as business requirements change, there may be newer requirements, such as to be able to analyze customer data along with the order details. To perform this new task without disturbing the existing architecture, a robust architecture has to be in place from the beginning. A neat ETL architecture allows the introduction of new data sources, without causing any friction to the existing solutions already in place.

ETL architecture consists of the stages through which the ETL process goes, as rendered in Figure 4-7.

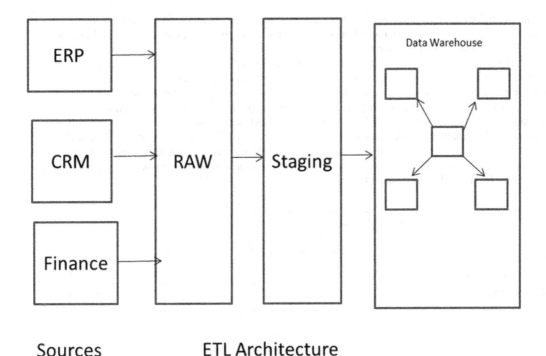

Sources   ETL Architecture

Figure 4-7. The ETL process, depicting how data is fetched from source systems and saved in a data warehouse, and the intermediate steps involved

There are usually three stages after the source system:

1. Raw

2. Staging

3. Data Warehouse

When fetching data from another business system such as ERP, CRM, or Finance, the first point of interaction is usually an FTP server, in which the flat files from the source systems are placed. The data from the flat files are read into raw tables that are an exact replication of the data in the source files.

The data from the raw tables is then cleansed and transported to the staging tables. Cleansing implies formatting the data types to a standardized format. For example, data formats from different source systems could be in different formats, or products could be defined in different ways in different source systems. The staging area takes care of applying such changes, to make the data ready for the onset of uniform business rules.

The next stage in the ETL architecture is the data warehouse. The data warehouse in the operational databases are normally relational: each table consists of attributes in columns and data values in rows. Different tables are joined to each other by relationships, such as one-to-one, one-to-many, or many-to-many, which allow combining of data in different tables. RDBMS (relational data base management systems) are designed for transactional systems and not for historical data storage. Being able to query historical data is not the only reason for transforming the transactional data into data warehouses. Integrating data from different business systems and, at the same time, storing historical events and transactions from every system requires a data warehousing solution.

The sharing of customer and sales data among business users is, for example, a case for a data warehouse solution. Data in the data warehouse is organized according to a dimensional model in a star schema. Star schemas are optimized for querying large data sets and are used in data warehouses and data marts to support BI and analytic applications and ad hoc queries for querying large data sets. Within the data warehouse or data mart, a dimension table is associated with a fact table by using a foreign key relationship. The dimension table has a single primary key that uniquely identifies each member record (row). The fact table contains the primary key of each associated dimension table as a foreign key. The fact tables contain the numeric measures, which are calculated fields such as sales, quantity, and total number of employees. The dimension tables contain attributes that reference the fact tables, such as geography, customer, product, etc. (see Figure 4-8). For example, sales data, such as revenue and quantity of products in the fact table, can be combined with product and geography dimension tables, to determine which products were sold and from which geographic location.

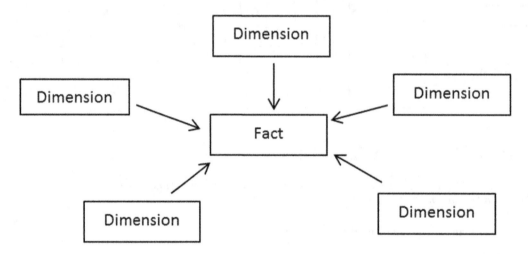

Figure 4-8. *A star schema with the fact table containing the numerical values and the attributes in the dimension tables*

Star Schema

A star schema, as in Figure 4-9, depicts the fact table, which contains numerical values, called measures, joined to dimension tables with a foreign key dependency. A foreign key dependency is a field one table that uniquely defines a row in another table. For example, the SalesPersonKey field in the Dimension table called DimSalesPerson points to the one or more rows in the fact table called FactSales. This dependency, in business terms, determines the total number of products sold by a particular salesperson.

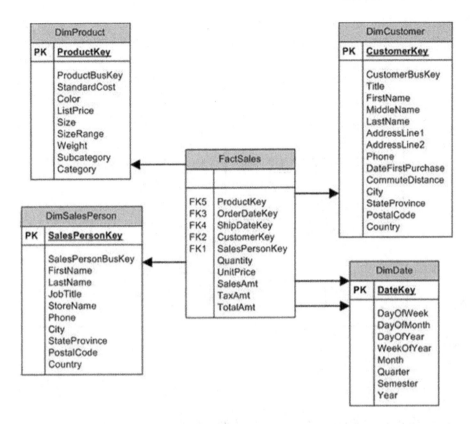

Figure 4-9. *The foreign key depencies between the dimension tables and fact table*

A star schema takes into account the different levels at which the measures have to be calculated. This is known as granularity. For example, in a star schema, Units_Sold can be calculated at day, week, month, quarterly, or year levels. Similarly, Units_Sold can be calculated at Store_Number, State_Province, and Country levels. Units_Sold, when combined with the Dim_Product table, can yield Units_Sold at Product, Brand, and Product category levels. The aggregation of the measures occurs at the hierarchical levels of the dimensions. Figure 4-10 shows the fact table, which contains such measures as Amount_Sold and Quantity_Sold. These measures can be calculated weekly, monthly, or yearly. The lowest granularity is that of a day, but the amount sold can also be aggregated to the yearly level.

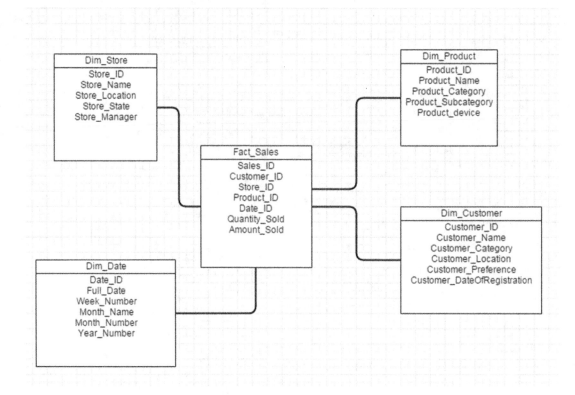

Figure 4-10. A star schema data model, also called a dimensional data model

Granularity in Dimensional Models

The design of a star schema also involves SCD (slowly changing dimensions), which maintain changes to the attributes in the dimension tables. For example, a customer may change her name. It is important to think about the change from a business perspective, if it is vital for the business to store all the changes occurring in the dimensions. In real-life implementation, not all the changes are important from a business intelligence point of view. It can be interesting for the business to know if a customer moves from one location to another or the name of a product changes, in order to keep track of the units sold for the product or customer details, regardless of name changes.

The challenge for data warehousing is, thus, to be able to cleanse, transform, and integrate data from multiple disparate sources that run on different technical platforms and sometimes in different geographical locations. Moreover, the data-warehousing solutions have to consider the business rules applied, the slowly changing dimensions, and the level of granularity required.

There are two approaches to data-warehousing architecture: Bill Inmon architecture and Ralph Kimball architecture. A stable and scalable data architecture based either on Ralph Kimball or Bill Inmon principles of data warehousing has to be in place to encompass ever-changing business needs. The method of architecture that should be chosen depends entirely on the business requirements and the data set-up. Bill Inmon advocates an enterprise data warehouse that is segmented into data marts, depending on the business intelligence needs for analysis per business area. The Bill Inmon approach is to store all the source data in an enterprise data warehouse by means of an ETL process (see Figure 4-11). The enterprise data warehouse data is then extracted and stored in smaller segments, called data marts, which serve specific business needs.

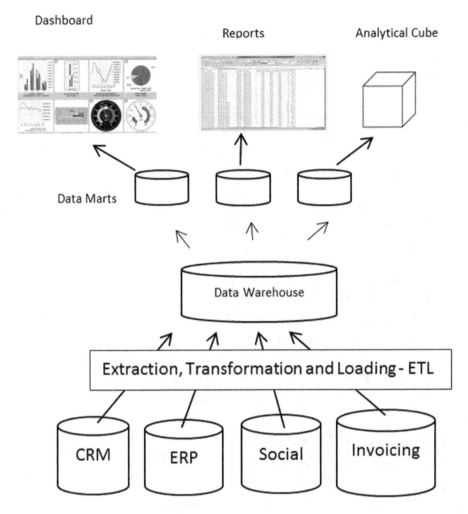

Figure 4-11. *The Bill Inmon architecture*

Ralph Kimball's approach preaches creation of the data marts initially, which then are merged into an enterprise-wide data warehouse, storing data catering to an entire organization (see Figure 4-12).

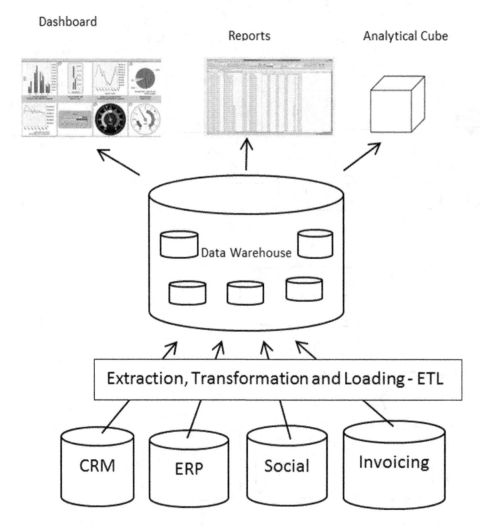

Figure 4-12. *The Ralph Kimball architecture*

Ralph Kimball advocates the dimensional model, consisting of a star schema, as discussed previously. The main advantage of a dimensional approach is that the data warehouse is easier for the end user to understand and to use. Also, the retrieval of data from the data warehouse tends to be quicker, due to fewer joins.

Key Features

ETL tools are not just meant to transfer data from a source system to a target system; they are used for integrating, profiling, validating, and consolidating data. SAP Data Services also has a built-in optimizer that actually analyzes the ETL jobs and pushes parts or the whole job to the database for processing, thereby load-balancing the job servers involved. If the Data Services job is using two source tables that belong to the same database schema and are connected by a join, the Data Services optimizer pushes the join condition to the database level, to fetch the data set that fulfills the condition. Data Services provides several functions for data cleansing and data validation. The data validation transformation is used to filter data according to certain given criteria.

Data validations can be tracked in pass or fail tables, to analyze the resulting data that ends up in the fail table, as in Figure 4-13, which shows a data flow design in Data Services Designer.

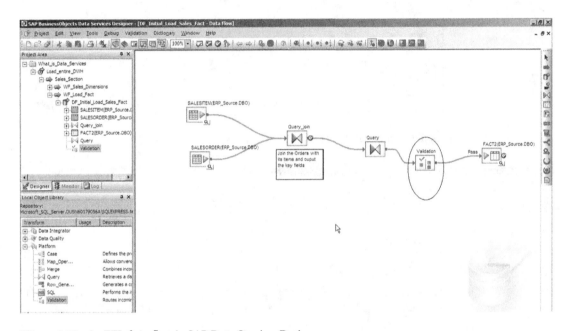

Figure 4-13. *An ETL data flow in SAP Data Services Designer*

Upon finding the reason for failure, the data can then be rectified and reloaded into the target data store.

As shown in Figures 4-14, 4-15, and 4-16, data validation rules can be handled in Data Services Designer very smoothly, by filtering rows that pass the validation rules and also raising alerts for data exceptions automatically. The rules can be specified, and the criteria for failure can be specified too, so when the data set does not meet the requirements, an exception is raised or e-mail sent. This functionality eases the process to manual interventions for data quality checks and exceptions.

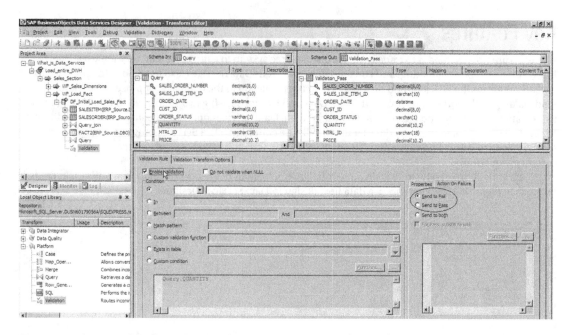

Figure 4-14. *An ETL data flow—data validation rule in SAP Data Services Designer*

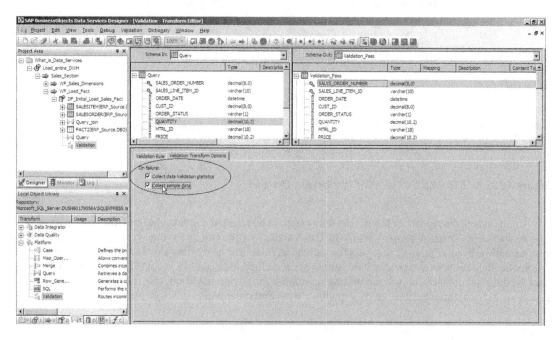

Figure 4-15. *An ETL data flow—validation transformation options in SAP Data Services Designer*

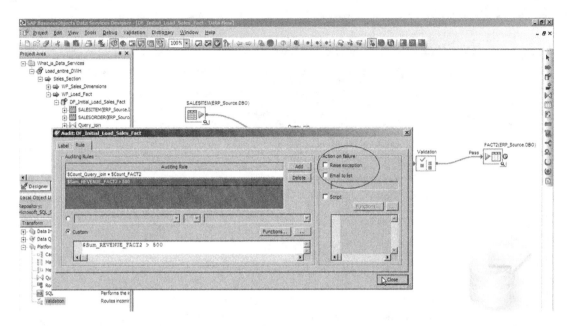

Figure 4-16. *Auditing rules can be configured in ETL data flow for data validation in SAP Data Services Designer*

Operational statistics about data validation can be collected for further analysis.

SAP Data Services provides an entire library of transformations for data integration, data quality, conditional formatting, and text data processing, as shown in Figure 4-17.

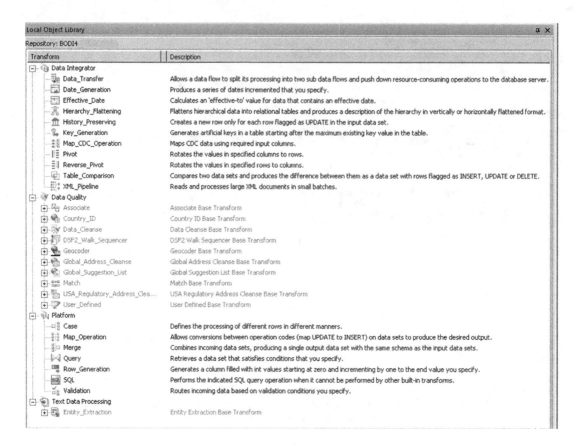

Figure 4-17. *The data transformation functions available in SAP Data Services Designer*

While running jobs in Data Services, the monitoring window, as shown in Figure 4-18, displays the status of the job run and also the statistics. The statistics displayed are very helpful in determining the time taken for each step in the process of extraction, transformation, and loading.

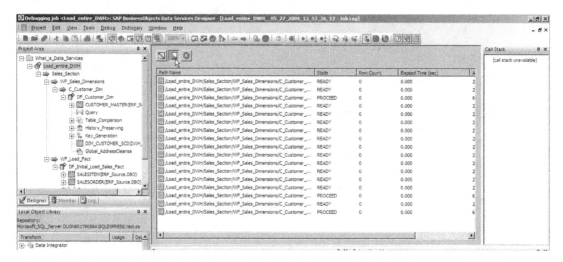

Figure 4-18. *The monitoring window in SAP Data Services Designer displaying the status of ETL jobs*

Data Services provides a tool, Data Services Object Promotion Management, which can be launched from the Administrator in the Data Services Management Console. It is a tool to promote objects and jobs between different environments, such as the development environment to the production environment. Administrators can transport the objects from a test to a development or to a production environment, using this tool to avoid overwriting and breaches in data security.

Data Services allows the creation of multiple file formats, using a wizard. Multiple delimited text files from either the job server or the local file system can be specified, and the wizard checks for multiple file format parameters for the row and column delimiters.

Technical Implementation Details

To be able to provide a secure and scalable Data Services and Information Steward environment, the following products have to be installed first:

- SAP Business Objects Information Platform Services (IPS), if you only want to use features of Data Services or Information Steward

- SAP Business Objects Business Intelligence platform (BI platform), if you also want to use Business Intelligence clients, such as Web Intelligence

These products provide platform services, such as SAP Data Services, use the SAP BusinessObjects Business Intelligence (BI) platform (or SAP BusinessObjects Information platform services) to exploit the scalable architecture that the platform provides. Server processes can be vertically scaled by running several, or all, server-side processes on one computer, for cost optimization, or horizontally scaled, by distributing the processes over a network of machines. Usually, multiple Data Services job servers or BI platform web applications are distributed on separate machines for load balancing and faster execution, thereby improving performance.

SAP Data Services Installation

Once the ETL architecture has been set up, the implementation has to begin. The ETL developers build the end-to-end data flow of extracting data from source systems, transforming it, and loading it into the data marts. This process requires meticulous planning, development, and testing for good end results. An iterative process—developing and testing the results in short repetitive steps to get the best outcome—is recommended.

At least three instances of SAP Data Services present an ideal choice to develop, quality-check, and promote jobs to production. ETL jobs are developed in the development environment, which, upon system testing, are promoted to the test environment. The test environment should hold a copy of production data, for accurate quality checks on the ETL data flows. To be more specific about the process of testing, a data reconciliation exercise has to be carried out to validate the raw data against the computed data in the data warehouse or data marts, after the transformations. A data reconciliation process should convey a high level of data accuracy, to consider the ETL architecture and development as a success.

Technical implementations of business intelligence or business analytics requirements begin with a business case, in which the business users likely want to analyze data from certain business areas. The next step is to capture the high-level requirements and prototype them, to get an approval on the agreement of the business case from the end users. Once the design is approved, the process of exploring the sourcing for such analytical dashboards or reports comes into the picture. As explained, the sourcing of data may not be a simple task. To analyze a business requirement may entail integrating two or more IT systems. This is where SAP Data Services plays an important role.

Because the data for the analytics dashboards and reports has to be up-to-date, the data content must be refreshed periodically. Some analytics solutions require weekly or monthly updates, but some may require the data to be refreshed daily. In order to automatize the data refresh, SAP Data Services has the functionality to schedule the ETL jobs in the Management Console. The jobs can, however, be run manually from within the Designer interface too. The Management Console interface also provides functionality to trace error messages in the logs, which is very helpful for debugging purposes (see Figure 4-19).

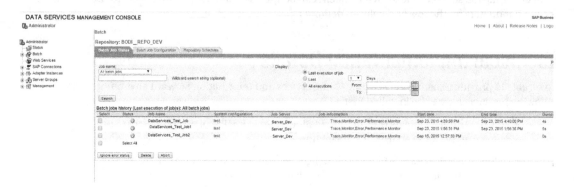

Figure 4-19. *The monitoring window in SAP Data Services Management Console*

Sample Implementation

After having gone through the technical advantages provided by SAP Data Services, let us focus on real-life examples of Data Services implementations. As the impact of monetization of data rises, so does the need to integrate heterogeneous data sources, to gain insights about the business performance metrics, customer behavior, and process optimization. Data for each business process does not necessarily reside on one technical platform, further complicating the process of integrating data sources. Businesses usually purchase several products to support one single purpose as ad hoc solutions, but soon enough, these ad hoc solutions turn into permanent solutions and have to be considered as sources during data consolidation.

Consider a telecom company, for example. Telcos typically have data in the following IT systems:

- *ERP*: ERP systems generally handle data pertaining to product planning, material purchasing, inventory control, distribution, accounting, marketing, finance, and HR. There are various software vendors that provide ERP products, such as SAP, Microsoft, Oracle, Infor, and Epicor.

- *CRM*: CRM products cater to a broad range of business needs, such as managing customer data, customer interaction, and customer and business support. Some of the CRM vendors in the market include Salesforce, Microsoft Dynamics, Netsuite, and Marketo.

- *Billing*: Billing handles the invoicing and revenue aspects of telecom operations. Common telecom billing software vendors are Single.eView, LogiSense, and Amdocs billing solutions.

- *Mediation*: Mediation systems are used to process call detail records (CDRs)for billing purposes. Data such as call duration, peak time, and call length are contained in CDRs.

Some use cases for data-driven marketing and sales include customer segmentation, to improve sales and satisfy more customers, and better and personalized tariff plans and credit scoring, to serve customers better at point-of-sale outlets.

The first business-use case—customer segmentation—requires not only gathering all customer-related data from the all the IT systems but also integrating market research data, to find patterns and trends in behavior analysis. Customer data resides in the ERP system for the products purchased by a customer, in the billing system for the invoicing, in the CRM system for the customer interactions with the company. Call detail records are stored in the mediation system and many other systems, such as order management, provisioning, etc.

In order to be able to segment the customer base, many factors have to be taken into account, and conditions must be determined for each segment, such as whether the segment will be based on geographic location, income category, or purchase capacity. Often, each segment has to contain detailed data regarding the most profitable customers and also potential customers, so that the latter can be converted into customers. The data from ERP, billing, and mediation reveals important aspects about the customer, such as the products owned, the billing history, how often the customer calls or messages, and at which times and from which destinations. If the market research data about customers' purchase history, income, and number of family members can be combined with the internal data, this can yield valuable insights into what kind of customers buy the most phones, call most, whether they use streaming services, and how much data they consume.

The different systems that contain a variety of data regarding the customer are

- *ERP*: Contains data about the product owned by the customer

- *CRM*: Maintains data about customer contact and interaction details

- *Customer Care systems*: Maintains data about customer complaints and interactions with the customer care

- *Billing*: Contains data about customer invoicing history

- *Mediation*: Maintains data about customer call details

- *Market research data*: The external data regarding individuals that companies usually buy from market research companies. This data is useful in terms of getting to know more about customers' socio-demographics, income, purchase history, etc.

To be able to blend data from internal IT systems and market research data, SAP Data Services is the tool that can consolidate data from all sources, using business rules and data-quality checks (see Figure 4-20).

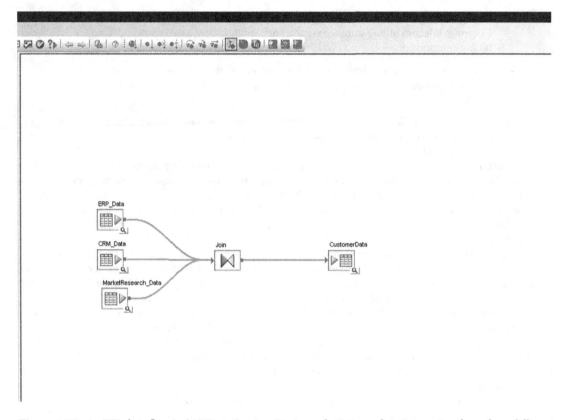

Figure 4-20. *An ETL data flow in SAP Data Services Designer depicting a data integration from three different source systems*

Data from each of the systems can be fetched in CSV (comma separated values) files and read into raw tables. The data in the raw tables should then be formatted and standardized to look as much alike as possible, to be able to consolidate. The data from stage tables should then be stored in the data warehouse in a star schema, for quick and easy access via BI analysis tools, to generate insights about business opportunities and market conditions.

The preceding process of data blending from different businesses can be defined in terms of the following steps:

1. Identify the goal and business gain of a business analytics initiative.

2. Determine the different milestones, and the deliverables in each of the milestones that contribute to the bigger roadmap.

3. Identify the business processes that are involved in each of these milestones.

4. Identify the supporting IT systems that support each of these business processes.

5. Identify the data requirements and the IT systems that can deliver the same.

6. Design the data architecture along with the data integrations required.

7. Determine the business rules required to transform the data to deliver the insights.

8. Build the data flows from source systems into the data warehouse.

9. Conduct tests and data quality checks to ensure the data integrations function as they should and that data integrity is maintained.

10. Gradually integrate all the data sources required in the entire business analytics project.

11. Operationalize the data flows between all the source systems, setting up alarms in case of data lapses.

12. Maintain the data quality and integrity in the data warehouse by operationalizing data checks.

Some measures that have to be taken care of in every aspect of a business analytics project are to maintain data quality and a shorter time to market. Early adoption of new business solutions is made easier with quicker deliveries, early on in the project.

The second case is that of credit scoring of customers before selling them a service or a handset, in the case of in telecom companies. To avoid fraudulent customers or bad debt, it is vital to do some background checks about the customer, before selling a service. To facilitate such functionality for sales representatives, there has to be a lot of work done in the background, involving BI. Data from billing reveals the invoicing and payment details of an existing customer, which, when matched with external data about credit history, generates insights about a customer's income, expenditures, loans, and derogatory information, if any. A credit score can be calculated based on a customer's financial and invoicing history, when aligned with business rules.

To be able to build a system that generates credit scoring requires consolidating data from billing, mediation, and external sources that generate an overall credit profile of customers. This, again, entails a similar architecture of source data and then the ETL architecture spanning raw, stage, and star schemas. In this case, however, it is vital to save historical data of customer credit reports and credit scores, to refer to a later stage. This would require implementing the SCD (slowly changing dimension), to be able to store all the historical stages of a customer's credit report and credit score.

The technical IT systems involved in such a credit scoring model are as follows:

- *ERP*: To check the current product owned by the customer and the product inventory

- *Billing*: To keep a check on past invoices or any reminders sent to customers

- *Point-of-sale (POS) systems*: The systems in stores in which sales agents place orders on behalf of customers or check inventory. The POS systems are connected to ERP systems.

- *External systems for credit history*: Credit history data is usually available in external systems that have consumer credit history data.

A customer inquiry to purchase a new product or service at a POS triggers a chain of processes, as illustrated in Figure 4-21. The POS communicates with the ERP system, to check the inventory for stock; the billing or invoicing system, for the customer's billing history; and the external credit history data, for the customer's historic credit data. The data from all the dependent systems are then sent to a credit scoring system, to deduce a score for the likelihood of a fraudulent customer.

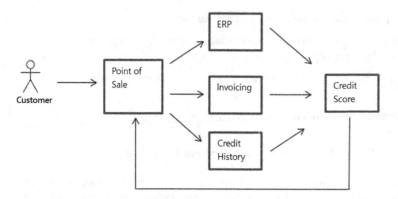

Figure 4-21. *The systems that communicate in the background when a customer makes an inquiry at a point of sale*

This score is then fed into the POS for the sales agent to decide whether to provide the customer with the desired service or product, depending on the customer's probability of becoming a defaulter.

While the use-case diagram in Figure 4-21 may appear simple, in reality, such a robust solution entails a great deal of data integration between several IT systems. In the case of a telecom company wanting to implement such a credit-scoring model, IT systems such as ERP, billing, and external systems that house credit history have to be integrated through SAP Data Services. Data from each of the systems can be fetched by delivering .csv files onto a File Transfer Protocol (FTP) server from the source systems.

As in Figure 4-22, the source IT systems deliver data in .csv files on FTP servers. At regular intervals, the ETL jobs run scripts that check the presence of the files on the server. If the files are not found under the designated directories, the scripts ensure that an error message gets logged in the server and checks again intermittently for new files. If the data files are found, the ETL job processes the files by cleansing, transforming, and loading them into the target systems, which, in this case, is the data warehouse. The data warehouse could be an Oracle data base or SQL server or any other database from any of the database vendors. The data from the data warehouse is then analyzed, using SAP Business Analytics dashboards or reporting solutions, to gather insights.

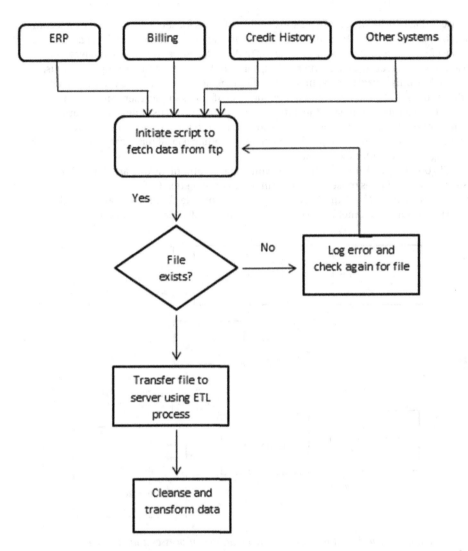

Figure 4-22. *A process for fetching from source systems files from the FTP server, via ETL jobs*

Taking the example of a credit score, data from the data warehouse is then uploaded into the POS system, using the same mechanism of .csv files on a FTP server. Once the data files from the data warehouse containing credit scores are placed on FTP servers, the POS system picks up the data files and uploads the data in the system, making the credit scores visible in the POS system for the salesperson in the store. Thus, a seemingly simple process involves several business processes and transcends several IT processes and systems, to deliver data and relevant information.

The third use case is that of designing more personalized tariff plans for services provided by telecom companies, in order to retain customers. To arrive at tariff plans that are more adapted to the customer needs, companies must first determine the customer needs. To do that, companies have to analyze customer call data and segment it according to their calling habits or Internet data-consumption habits. Data regarding call detail records reveal important insights about the destinations that a certain segment of customers call, the time they call, and the duration that they call. If, for example, there are certain segments of customers that call abroad most of the time, then providing these customers with a tariff plan with reduced call charges for abroad will help improve customer retention. There could be other customers who call most frequently within the family. For such a segment, providing a tariff plan that allows reduced charges for family calling would definitely keep interest.

As in Figure 4-23, in order to work out personalized campaigns or tariff plans that are targeted for certain customer segments, companies must get to know their customer better. Getting to know the customer better can only be achieved by gathering as much data as possible about the customer and analyzing the same to understand customer behavior, demographics, preferences, and the risk to churn.

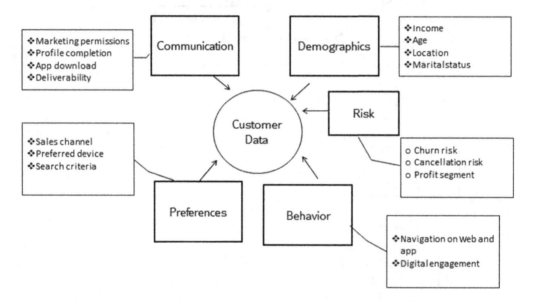

Figure 4-23. *Gathering a holistic view of customer data from all business processes and IT systems*

In order to gain more insights into customer calling habits, data from ERP, invoicing systems, and CRM has to be blended with the CDR (call detail record) data. ERP, invoicing, and CRM data generate insights about the customer's current tariff plan, the customer's handset, and invoicing details, while the CDR data generates insights about the actual calling details. Integrating the preceding systems involved can help in categorizing customers into frequent callers, frequent message senders, customers who mostly call abroad, or customers who mostly use their phones to access the Internet. To integrate data from different source systems, ETL processes have to fetch the source data, transform it into standard formats that make data matching possible, and, finally, store the data in a data warehouse. Data from the source systems are extracted using ETL tools such as SAP Data Services, then cleansed and formatted in several steps, such as those known as raw and stage. The cleansed and transformed data is then stored in data warehouses or data marts for further consumption through reports and dashboards, thereby shielding business users from behind-the-scene technical complications.

With all the advantages that SAP Data Services provides for data cleansing, transformation, and integration, it is an optimal tool for data integration purposes. As in Figure 4-24, data from source systems is fetched using SAP Data Services, by fetching files from an FTP server.

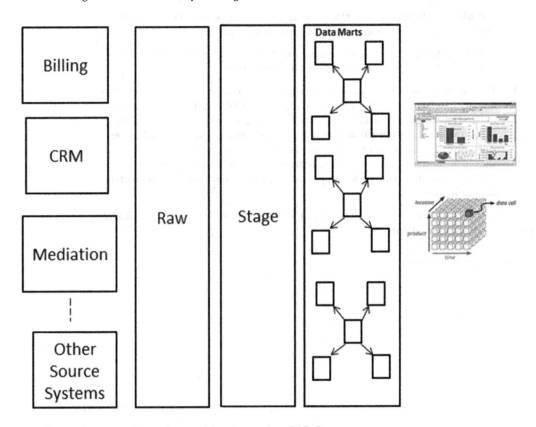

Extraction, transformation and loading using SAP Data Services

Figure 4-24. An ETL data flow facilitating end-to-end data flow

Following are the steps involved in ETL processes:

1. The ETL architecture has to be defined with all the data integration points taken into account.

2. The frequency of data loads has to be defined in accordance with how often the data from the source system is likely to be refreshed.

3. The data warehouse and data mart design has to be finalized before the ETL processes begin.

4. The business rules that determine the business logic that should be built into the ETL flows should be decided in conjunction with business users.

5. Data formatting rules should also be defined, along with business user inputs, for example, whether all phone numbers should be prefixed with a country code.

6. Once all the data formatting and business logic and the design of target data stores, such as the data marts, are defined, the ETL work flow build in SAP Data Services can start.

7. The ETL work flows, once developed, should be tested for data reconciliation and data quality and stress-tested for performance testing.

8. Data from the data marts and data warehouses can be checked by business users with any of the SAP Business Analytics suite of products.

9. The rule of thumb for any SAP Data Services ETL implementation is to make sure that all the integrations with source system are established and stress-tested in the first layer, which is called the raw layer or the ingestion layer. The next layer, called the staging or transformation layer, transforms data, by applying business rules. The third and final layer, which is the data mart or data warehouse layer, should be designed keeping in mind reporting and dashboarding needs. The ability to drill up and down data depends on the granularity levels defined in the data warehouse.

Chapter 7 will elaborate the details of an end-to-end business analytics project, from requirement to architecture to analytics solutions.

CHAPTER 5

■ ■ ■

SAP BusinessObjects BI Platform

Today, owing to businesses' expanding online presence, there is an abundance of data. More and more consumers use mails and chats for communication and online services to book taxis and flights and tables at restaurants. All of this commerce relies on IT services, and, in order to optimize this technology, businesses must be able to evaluate their processes by visualizing information.

Businesses run on information, which is facilitated by IT systems, in the form of dashboards and reports. Business users are able to take strategically correct decisions regarding business investments or engagements, based on data. Data has always been vital to business, but in today's connected world, we are inundated with ever-increasing amounts of data. It becomes imperative to empower business users with data, which is diverse and huge in volume, in a simple manner. Business users should be able to use data to gain insights into their business, and in the least amount of time possible.

Story-telling through data is what appeals to decision makers; data is not just about statistics. Because companies have realized the value of data, most businesses gather as much of it as possible, for use when the need arises. Easy availability of data leads to expectations within the business side of a company about insights gained from data. It is usually the responsibility of the IT department to convert raw data into information and to distribute the same within the organization, thereby raising awareness of data and promoting knowledge-sharing through collaboration among departments. In recent years, mobile solutions have seen a steep rise in popularity. This makes it vital that business analytics solutions be mobile-friendly, thereby making data available to business users on the go.

Introduction to the SAP BusinessObjects BI Platform

For a business analytics tool to be effective, it should have the attributes discussed in the following list.

- An intuitive, easy-to-use interface with drag-and-drop features to facilitate your data-driven decision making

- Easy traceability of communication, inquiries/disputes, splits, adjustments, and more

- Ease of use and the ability to distribute data to a wide audience through reports, dashboards, analytics, and self-service business intelligence (BI). Self-service BI lets users create their own reports for analysis purposes, rather than wait for IT to help them.

© Sudipa DuttaRoy 2016
S. DuttaRoy, *SAP Business Analytics*, DOI 10.1007/978-1-4842-1383-4_5

- Routine BI reports have to be refreshed every day, to reflect updated and fresh data. Instead of manually refreshing the data, reports can be scheduled to run during the night, or before office hours begin, so that business users have reports with updated data at the start of the day. It is important to automatize processes, such as scheduling, to reduce administration costs. Some business analytics tools use third-party scheduling tools to automate running such tasks as running ETL (extraction, transformation, and loading) processes, to extract and load data into data warehouses or refreshing reports. It's always better to choose a business analytics tool that has built-in scheduling features, so that an IT department does not have to maintain yet another system, i.e., scheduling tool.

- With the increase in the number of business processes being tracked, the number of IT systems that support such processes also increases. The amount of data from each such system increases too, resulting in problems with data storage and performance issues. If data retrieval is not optimized, it could result in high data latency. It is vital to choose a business analytics tool that scales and supports high performance and faster data retrieval, to cope with an ever-growing amount and variety of data.

- Business intelligence tools that have an open architecture integrate better with other platforms and software solutions. Open architecture reduces a product's time to market by reducing the implementation time, to integrate a new business analytics solution into an existing ecosystem.

- BI solutions to be implemented must have the flexibility to connect to a wide range of databases. Some BI solutions support databases from the same vendor, making it difficult for organizations to implement such solutions. Business analytics tools that are widely sought after have the capability to fetch data from multiple sources of data. As new databases emerge at an increasing rate, compatibility with a wide variety of databases becomes more important. Popular databases that are used by most organizations include Oracle, Microsoft SQL Server, MySql, HANA, IBM DB2, SAP Sybase, PostgreSQL, Teradata, Amazon Simple DB.

- As more and more organizations want to be pro-active rather than reactive in their approach to customer engagement, real-time data insights are imperative. Business analytics tools should be able to handle real-time analytics. A lack of real-time data hinders decision making and greatly limits the advantages of BI.

- Some BI applications require embedding or integrating data or charts from other applications. Good BI tools make this process simple and flexible to save time on re-creating the data flows from scratch.

- Modern BI tools must support all devices and platforms. BI applications must provide a seamless experience for business users, irrespective of device.

- Operational reporting capabilities designed to support the day-to-day activities of the organization, often scheduled to run nightly and delivered via e-mail or refreshed on portals, are an important consideration. If a BI tool does not support the preceding functionality and requires purchasing additional software to support e-mail and scheduling, this results in additional costs for the company.

The SAP BusinessObjects BI platform provides IT departments with an effective means of sharing BI content across an entire organization, empowering business users to deep dive into data, in order to make informed decisions.

The BI platform is used to gain access to the data discovery, dashboards, and reporting features of an organization. It is a one-stop platform for the organization to distribute information to a wide audience of business users.

The following are solution capabilities provided by the SAP BI platform:

- *Data discovery—SAP Lumira*: SAP Lumira is a data discovery tool that makes combining and visualizing data from multiple sources very easy. Lumira provides data-preparation features to edit data, transpose values, rename certain attributes, create variables, or create hierarchies in the data set before the data can be visualized. Business users of all skill levels can prepare, visualize, and analyze the data to identify trends and patterns, with minimum IT help. SAP Lumira can be set up on-premise, in the cloud, or on the Web.

- *Reporting—SAP Crystal Reports, SAP BusinessObjects Web Intelligence, and SAP BusinessObjects Explorer*: Ad hoc and scheduled reporting capabilities are provided to business users to deliver meaningful insights that provide real value of data, which is consolidated from several IT systems, to business users. Simple to understand yet pixel perfect data visualizations that are able to be shared with external customers or partners are a key feature of SAP Business Analytics reporting tools.

- *Business intelligence platform—SAP BusinessObjects BI Platform, SAP BusinessObjects Analysis edition for Microsoft, and SAP BusinessObjects Analysis edition for OLAP*: BI platform tools provide reliable self-service access to BI data by business users. The BI platform is able to distribute data fast and smoothly to a wide business audience.

- *Mobile analytics solutions—Analytics apps*: SAP BI analytics mobile solutions allow business users to tap into the data, on the move. Mobile analytics also makes access to data seamless.

The SAP BI platform shields business users from the complexities of data, providing ready-to-use business intelligence data insights. The semantic layer between the data sources and the business layers handles the data transformations, making it easier for business users. The semantic layers can manage a variety of data types and data sources from different database providers.

The SAP BI platform can use single sign on to login to several BI tools, making the experience seamless for users of the platform. The BI tools access control, and access to source database connections can also be managed on a single BI platform. Figure 5-1 shows a login screen for the SAP BI platform.

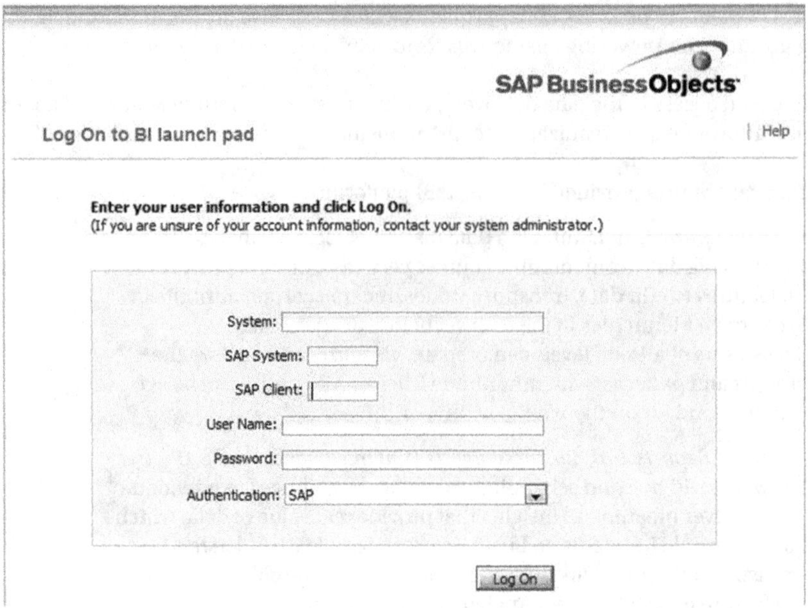

Figure 5-1. *The SAP BusinessObjects BI platform login page*

In Figure 5-2, the SAP Business Analytics tools that are available within the SAP BI platform are displayed on the far right side. The advantage of accessing tools through the SAP BI platform is that users can manage their tools through a single sign on and data security can be centrally managed through the CMC (Central Management Console).

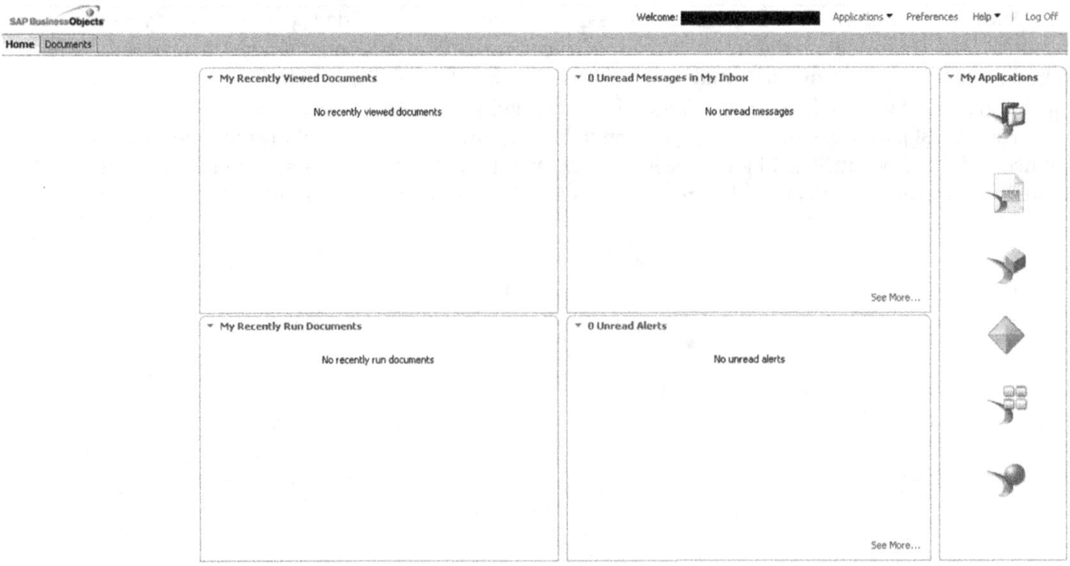

Figure 5-2. *SAP BI launchpad*

Key Features

The SAP BusinessObjects BI platform provides many proven solutions that cater to key performance indicators (KPIs) driving business goals. In order to provide a scalable, efficient, and fast-performing platform, the SAP BusinessObjects BI platform is supported by a robust architecture in the background.

The SAP BI platform is supported by two main BI servers: the Adaptive Processing Server (APS) and the Adaptive Job Server (AJS). Much of the behind-the-scenes work done to support the BI platform is performed by the Adaptive Processing Server and the Adaptive Job Server.

The SAP BusinessObjects Business Intelligence platform can be thought of as a series of conceptual tiers.

Client Tier

The client tier is comprised of the desktop client applications that interact with the SAP BusinessObjects BI platform to provide a variety of reporting, analytic, and administrative capabilities. Examples include the Central Configuration Manager (CCM), Information Design Tool, and SAP Crystal Reports.

Web Tier

The web tier, consisting of web applications deployed to a Java web application server, provides SAP BusinessObjects BI platform functionality to end users through web browsers. Web tier examples include applications such as the Central Management Console and BI launchpad. Web Services, a part of the web tier, provides SAP BusinessObjects BI platform services, such as session authentication, user privilege management, scheduling, search, administration, reporting, and query management functionality, to software tools, via the web application server. An example is Live Office.

Management Tier

The management tier, which is the main tier and, therefore, also known as the intelligence tier, handles all the components that make up SAP BusinessObjects BI platform. The management tier consists of the Central Management Server (CMS) and the Event Server and associated services. The CMS contains configuration, auditing, and operation information. The Central Configuration Management also serves as a platform-management tool. Server Intelligence Agent (SIA) is responsible for starting the CMS. The servers responsible for the BI platform can be managed from within the CMS and the CCM. Figure 5-3 shows the how the SIA can be managed from the CCM.

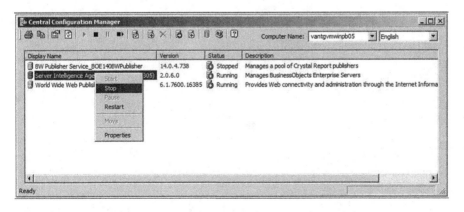

Figure 5-3. *The Central Configuration Manager (CCM)*

Storage Tier

The storage tier consists of the IFRS (Input File Repository System) and the OFRS (Output File Repository System), which handle the storing of reports and scheduled instances. The IFRS manages files that contain information pertaining to reports, such as the following file types: `.rpt`, `.car`, `.exe`, `.bat`, `.js`, `.xls`, `.doc`, `.ppt`, `.rtf`, `.txt`, `.pdf`, `.wid`, `.rep`, and `.unv`. The OFRS stores the report scheduled instances created by the system, such as the following file types: `.rpt`, `.csv`, `.xls`, `.doc`, `.rtf`, `.txt`, `.pdf`, `.wid`, and `.rep`. The storage tier also manages server cashing, to reduce the I/O, for optimal server usage.

Processing Tier

The processing tier accesses data in databases to produce reports. The processing tier consists of the APS (Adaptive Processing Server), which is responsible for any post-processing of a publication job, including PDF merging and publication extension, and the AJS (Adaptive Job Server) is responsible for the Scheduling and Publishing Service.

Data Tier

The data tier contains data for BI reports, for example, report data in relational databases, OLAP data sources, and the actual universe files (`.unx` and `.unv`) or system databases for the CMS, Auditing Data Store, Lifecycle management console, and Monitoring application.

Central Management Console

Most of the administrative operations for the BI platform are carried out in the web-based tool known as the Central Management Console (CMC). Some of the tasks that can be managed in the CMC are user creation, user group creation, server management, content promotion from test or development environment to production environments, and configuration of security settings. The CMC can also be used to customize the BI launchpad.

Administrators can log on to the CMC to manage user groups and granted rights. Administrators can assign access rights to users or user groups at folder level, universe level, or database connection level.

Server management is also done through the CMC. A group of servers run under a single SIA on a host. Servers can be created, stopped, and restarted in the CMC. In Figure 5-4, the CMC home page displays all the functionalities available within CMC.

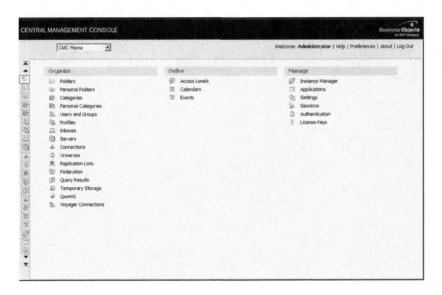

Figure 5-4. *CMC home page*

Technical Implementation Details

The technical functioning of a BI platform implementation depends on the number of users that will access the platform, the number of client tools that must be made available, and the number of source systems to be integrated.

The types of BI platform users are as follows:

- *Information consumers*: Information consumers are the BI platform users who require data in the form of PDFs or Excel, delivered to a portal or their mailboxes. Information users do not have to create their own reports or make changes to existing reports. This type of user can be classified as Reader Only.

- *Business users*: Business users are those who sometimes create simple reports or make adjustments in existing reports, to suit their requirements. Business users cannot perform complex tasks.

- *Expert users*: Expert users are usually the BI developers who are able to create reports from scratch and carry out heavy-duty development, both on the semantic layers and reporting and dashboard tools.

The number of users who need access will have to be defined by the license management. The number of servers required to support the BI platform depends on the number of tools that are made available through the tool (each service supported by a few number of servers), the number of users that have to access the platform, and the amount of content. The IFRS and OFRS sizes have to be adjusted according to the size of the content. If many users have to access the platform concurrently, the SAP BI platform-sizing guide should be used to derive the correct size and number of servers, to provide a robust, scalable platform. Figure 5-5 shows the server management functionalities provided in CMC, namely, configuring, starting, and stopping the servers for each service.

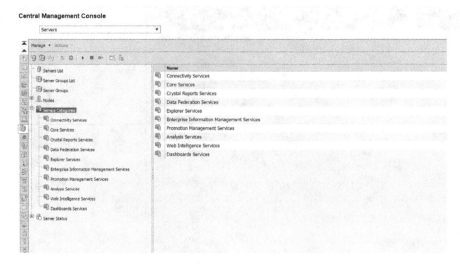

Figure 5-5. *Server management features in CMC*

Example of Implementation

The BI platform is, as has been stated, a one-stop platform for a variety of BI tools available to business users for business intelligence, including data discovery, reporting, dashboards, and scheduling. The BI platform handles the user access and security aspects of data in a very smooth manner.

New users can be added and access levels assigned to them individually or added to user groups. User groups can be created with certain access levels, to make it easier to add users at the group level. Figure 5-6 shows user- and access-level management features provided by the CMC. New user groups can be defined, and users added to them, and access levels provided to user groups, or users can be edited from within the CMC.

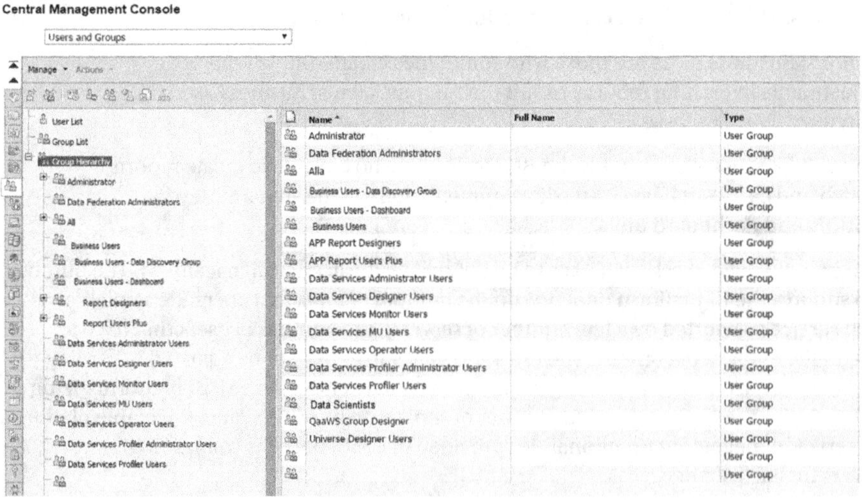

Figure 5-6. *Central Management Console—Users and Groups*

Organizations that start with a BI implementation usually start at a small scale, but as the volume of data grows over time, so does the number of source business systems that have to be integrated and the number of users who require access to the BI platform. In order to streamline the data-access process, there has to be a proper scalable data strategy in place, which is easily achieved when

- The amount of data increases

- The number of data sources increases

- The number of new users increases

The SAP BI platform is a gateway to a number of BI tools that can be made available through a single BI platform.

Several needs inform business users' ability to make good business decisions, such as data discovery, scheduled reports, or dashboards to check trends.

Let us consider an example of a train operator organization. A train operator has several processes involved within the business, each having unique needs and IT processes. There are also some business requirements that can be met by blending data from various systems. A train operator normally has a finance department, a ticketing system in which tickets are booked to keep track of sales, campaign systems that manage campaigns, social media management systems, and systems that manage the train timetables. Following are some typical business requirements:

- Keeping track of the sales by following up on the number of tickets sold, the amount of food and drinks sold on board, and revenue generation through partnerships

- Accounting and financial management

- Keeping track of train timetables, trends pertaining to train punctuality, track quality, number of maintenance checks carried out

- Inventory control for onboard services

- Social media management dashboards

In order to fulfill the preceding business requirements, an SAP BI implementation with tools that uniquely cater to each of the requirements should be implemented. SAP Lumira is a tool used for data discovery, to gain insights about data by easy drag-and-drop and self-service mechanisms.

SAP BusinessObjects Explorer and Web Intelligence are the tools for ad hoc and scheduled reports that are required by business users on a timely basis, to follow up on finance and accounting or customer acquisitions.

SAP Dashboards are used to display trends in regard to the number of customers acquired, sales figures, train punctuality, onboard sales, etc. SAP Dashboards is a great tool for data visualization and creating interactive dashboards. The dashboards connect to various data sources to display data, using various components, such as charts, graphs, and buttons, to help the dashboard consumer identify trends and make informed business decisions.

In the background, the data sources could be SAP BW running on SAP HANA, which is connected through a Bex connector in the IDT (Information Design Tool), or any other database, such as Oracle or SQL Server.

The BI platform in this example shields the business users from the complexities of the data sources, the connections required, and the underlying server architecture, thereby allowing them to focus on business goals. The BI platform has various servers in place to support the BI client tools, such as Dashboards, Web Intelligence, Lumira, Crystal Reports, and Explorer. The users and user groups are managed by the SAP BI platform on a single platform that leads to data access to various client tools, thereby easing the process for both business users and an IT department.

An SAP BI implementation in the preceding case can be elaborated as follows:

1. The project should be initiated with a business case outlining the business gains of a business analytics implementation.

2. Once the business case has been defined with the goals in mind, the goals can be defined as targets during different milestones.

3. In order to achieve the milestones in an analytics project, the data required to achieve the target, the tools required, and the team that will execute the implementation have to be defined and in place.

4. The data visualization requirements have to be analyzed to be able to choose the tool that is best suited for a particular requirement. For example, SAP BusinessObjects Web Intelligence is a good tool for static reports, while SAP Analysis is good for ad hoc analysis that business users can carry out themselves

5. The ETL architecture and the business rules for data cleansing, formatting, and loading have to be defined early on in the process, to ensure data availability for analytics.

6. The financial data from SAP BW, social media data, data from booking systems, data from ancillaries, data from partner sites, etc., has to extracted from the source systems and loaded into a data warehouse. The data warehouse could be an Oracle or Microsoft SQL Server or SAP HANA, or any other vendor database, based on the business requirements. The data in the data warehouse is stored in star schemas, as in Figure 5-7, to facilitate data visualization in business analytics tools.

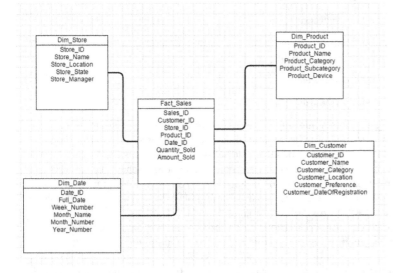

Figure 5-7. *A star schema design with fact and dimension tables*

Business analytics tools are a means of achieving the goal of spreading knowledge and democratizing data within an organization. The key factors that facilitate this, however, are having a well-thought-out business analytics strategy roadmap and defining a winning business analytics team that will execute the strategy.

A Business Analytics Strategy Roadmap

For a business analytics implementation to be successful at an enterprise level, a business analytics strategy defining the goals, the milestones, roles, and business processes that need to be taken into account has to be defined first, before deciding on the tool set for implementation. A business analytics strategy should be designed to be agile and adaptive and as a continuous process for improvement.

A business analytics initiative in an organization starts with creating a business case outlining the business gain of such an implementation and the factors that facilitate a successful implementation, as in Figure 5-8. The business case, when approved by the CIO or CTOs after careful scrutiny, leads to a business analytics strategy roadmap definition.

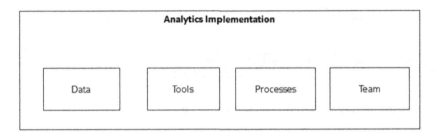

Figure 5-8. *The factors that define a successful business analytics strategy*

A more detailed business analytics plan, stemming from the overall strategy defining the data, tools, processes, and deliverables at every stage of the project, has to be defined, as in Figure 5-9. This plan can then be refined, to further break down the deliverables into small iterations of development and testing.

Business Analytics Plan

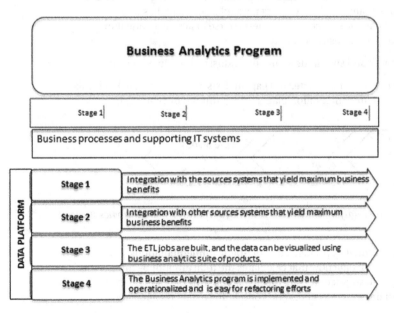

Figure 5-9. *A high-level business analytics plan*

A business analytics strategy should be aligned with the overall enterprise strategy, to deliver value to the business and to the customers. There are certain proven practices that have been widely accepted in the BI field, and organizations can take advantage of these best practices by tweaking and implementing those bits that suit their business. These can serve as broad guidelines, in terms of things to do and things to avoid for ensuring success of the BI initiative.

Tasks to ensure success of the BI strategy include the following:

- Creating a business case and outlining the expected advantages of each project, as in Figure 5-10

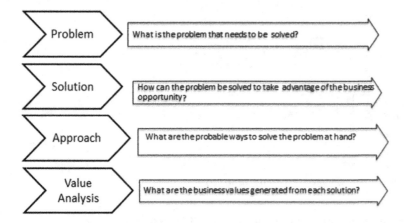

Figure 5-10. Creating a business case for a business analytics implementation

- Obtaining buy-in from stakeholders is vital, not only to find a sponsor for the business case, but also to make the business side adapt to the BI implementation. Each of the solution streams, and the value generated from them, has to be presented to the stakeholders, to choose the best course of action, taking into account the time to market, cost, and agility.

- Adapting best practices and standards within the industry domain in question

- Performing a current state, future state, and gap analysis, which in turn will serve as the foundation for a BI implementation plan, as diagrammed in Figure 5-11

Figure 5-11. Business analytics gap analysis, which serves as the foundation of an analytics strategy

- Taking actionable and small steps, instead of big-bang implementations. For example, building an ETL data flow that calculates the total amount by multiplying the units sold with the unit price. Testing the preceding workflow should include checking the data in the source systems and conducting a data reconciliation.

- Defining data and business rules governance, for example, maintaining the master data for products in one master data source to avoid duplicate and redundant data sources. It should be mandatory to define each product in a product master, along with all its attributes, for consumption across an enterprise, using this as the single version of truth.

- Using an iterative implementation approach, testing every step. It is very important to unit-test every analytics development, before testing the integration with other data flows. If the individual data flows do not function well, overall data quality suffers.

- Working with frameworks and adopting proven methodologies, not by the book, but by making adjustments to suit each organization's business needs

- Identifying related gaps and issues that hinder the BI implementation from creating value

- Documenting and analyzing the constraints and assumptions that are considered while designing a business analytics strategy. The assumptions can change in the future, thereby changing the circumstance of implementation of a strategy and giving rise to new opportunities that will have to be addressed.

The potential issues that have to be avoided when designing a business analytics strategy are as follows:

- It is never advisable to build data silos and person dependency, meaning that team members should be able to step into each other's roles and perform the tasks, which can be achieved by knowledge-sharing.

- A bigbang implementation approach is seldom a successful implementation plan. It has been proven that an iterative implementation, by incorporating the business users' feedback into the implementation early on, works best.

- A business analytics roadmap document stating the present and future goals should be the basis of a BI strategy. It is not commendable to set on a business analytics implementation path without a business analytics roadmap.

- A business analytics strategy must not only focus on data integration and stateof-theart BI tools. A business analytics strategy should be comprehensive enough, including team structure, responsibility sharing, and division of work.

- A business analytics strategy should not be inflexible. Businesses change their business processes pretty often, and having a rigid business analytics framework will make it very difficult for the business analytics team and tools to adapt to the changes. A business analytics strategy should be constantly tuned and adjusted to reflect the changing needs of a business.

An asis state should be analyzed to identify problem areas and arrive at a tobe plan. Only then should an analytics implementation plan be designed. An ideal plan should account for the capacity of both human and software resources such as servers, system performance, data quality, data security, metadata control, and data-retention policies. For example, highlevel decisions made about data retention impacts data architecture, such as partitioning of the data, as well as technical architecture, such as disk storage. More detailed decisions regarding whether all or most of the logic that corresponds to business rules should be handled in ETL or in reports has to be outlined, to develop solutions that are uniform across an enterprise.

The next section describes the structure and functioning of a business analytics team, which is one of the most vital aspects of an analytics implementation.

A Typical BI Team Structure

An efficient BI team consists of both technical and business analysts, who help implement the business analytics strategy roadmap. By utilizing business and technical experts together, outcomes can generally be met sooner and more accurately than if the teams were separate.

As in Figure 5-12, it is vital to clarify and define the team structure, roles, responsibilities, and deliverables expected from each team member. This not only ensures right balance of work distribution but also helps seal loopholes, if any, in terms of skillsets.

Role	• Clearly define the roles and skillset required
Accountabilities	• Define the responsibilities that come along with each role
Deliverables	• Define the key deliverables expected from each team member in each milestone
Cross Team Collaboration	• Define the roles and responsibilities in a cross-team collaboration, to avoid confusion

Figure 5-12. *Key steps in defining an analytics team structure*

Following are the main roles and responsibilities of a business analytics team:

- *Business analysts*: They are the bridge between the BI and business teams, such as marketing, sales, or pricing teams

- *Business subject matter experts*: These are the people in the organization who work on the source systems, such as marketing, sales, invoicing, and are business-oriented, therefore being knowledgeable about business data. Typical examples of such team members are business controllers.

- *Solution architects*: These are the professionals in charge of the design of the data warehouse and the technical setup of the business analytics implementation

- *ETL developers*: These are team members, specializing in ETL, who understand the organizational data and build ETL solutions to achieve business insights.

- *Report developers*: These team members develop reports and dashboards to visualize data.

- *Data analysts*: These are the team members responsible for analyzing data, in order to provide business insights, by having a thorough understanding of business processes and business data. Business analysts also make good data analysts.

The preceding roles do not have to be assumed by entirely different people. A solution architect can also function as an ETL developer and/or data analyst, thereby spreading knowledge within the organization.

A BI team not only works on new development to meet new business requirements but also has to maintain the BI operations on a day-to-day basis, for example, ensuring the nightly ETL loads and running the reports and dashboards to refresh data. Some organizations have separate teams that take care of BI operations and BI development. But it is good practice to rotate the team members within both teams, to encourage the spread of knowledge. Peer design review meetings are a good way to spread knowledge and get feedback on architecture and data flow designs.

A BI team needs to adapt to the best of the best practices within the field of analytics, gaining knowledge and reducing latency in delivering business value.

A successful business analytics implementation relies not only on the tools, processes, and technical architecture but mainly on the overall business analytics strategy and the roadmap defined before the inception of the analytics implementation.

CHAPTER 6

■ ■ ■

SAP Analytics Products

In this chapter, you will learn about the various SAP Business Analytics offerings and the business cases for the same. While there are myriad business analytics tools, each tool is best suited to a particular use case.

Introduction to Each Product

Analytics helps to unlock the real value of business data. Data monetization is a very important aspect of today's digital business. In order to gain the maximum possible advantage from a business's key performance indicators, the business data has to be blended with data from several source systems, to be analyzed and generate value that leads to reduced churn, better customer experience, and increased revenue.

As illustrated in Figure 6-1, the parameters that define the success rate of business analytics implementations or practices depend on various factors—from defining the overall goal and strategy to understanding the business requirements and finding the right skills for their implementation.

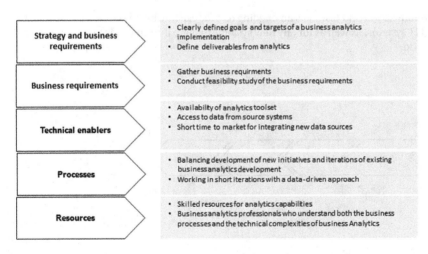

Overview of critical success factors in a Business Analytics

Strategy and business requirements	• Clearly defined goals and targets of a business analytics implementation • Define deliverables from analytics
Business requirements	• Gather business requirments • Conduct feasibility study of the business requirements
Technical enablers	• Availability of analytics toolset • Access to data from source systems • Short time to market for integrating new data sources
Processes	• Balancing development of new initiatives and iterations of existing business analytics development • Working in short iterations with a data-driven approach
Resources	• Skilled resources for analytics capabilities • Business analytics professionals who understand both the business processes and the technical complexities of business Analytics

Figure 6-1. *The critical factors that define the success rate of business analytics*

Be it media, gaming or financial industries, every organization should be able to leverage data to keep a check on key performance indicators, preferably in real time. Gone are the days of running batch jobs to update data warehouses that stored historical transactional data. To be able to gain maximum output from analytics solutions, organizations have to integrate several disparate systems to gain a 360-degree view of their business and customers. For example, to check the value of an entire customer life cycle—the complete customer journey from acquisition through all transactions the customer has had with the company—demands analysis. To analyze the entire customer journey, data from such systems as ERP, CRM, customer service, and billing and invoicing must be integrated. Some business requirements are business-critical and demanding, which makes it even more important that data be of a high quality, available, and fast to query.

Simple, easy-to-understand data visualization is the demand of the day. C-level executives need a beautiful interface with dashboards projecting the KPIs (key performance indicators) that drive business goals, while financial analysts have to dig into data and analyze and crunch the numbers themselves. The SAP BI Analytics toolset has a solution for every analytics need, be it storytelling through data, pixel-perfect reports for external partners, or invoices sent to customers.

Business analytics is a continuous method to optimize business processes, improve business efficiency, and aid revenue generation. Because it is a continuous process, the iteration cycle has to be repeated over and over. A business analytics process is mainly composed of the following stages (also see Figure 6-2):

- Define the problem or the goal of the project

- Gather data by means of data integrations and ETL work flows

- Use some of the SAP Business Analytics suite of products to visualize the data

- Analyze the data to deduce the factors that lead to insights

- Execute insights generation, to understand the customer base and the product sales figures

- Optimize the processes that lead to better business performance, based on the insights generated by business analytics initiatives

- Once the business processes are optimized, the response from them should undergo the same process cycles: gather data, analyze it to understand how the process transformations have fared, and optimize them further.

- This cycle of optimization and testing is an ongoing one for existing business processes and IT systems, as well as for any new systems that are introduced into a business scenario.

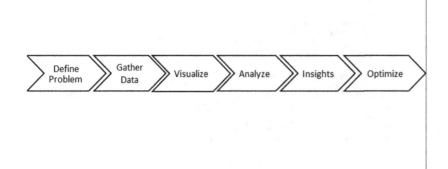

Figure 6-2. The process cycle for a business analytics implementation

SAP Business Analytics tools support the preceding expedient way of functioning at an enterprise level by providing quick time-to-market solutions. SAP BI tools are always updated with the latest patches, to keep them in sync with the latest market requirements, and all the tools are backward compatible, with previous versions to facilitate transitions to newer platforms. SAP BI has a neat licensing model, making it simple to purchase new or similar-but-upgraded versions of a business analytics product.

The SAP Business Analytics product portfolio is classified into reporting, discovery and analysis, dashboards and applications, and office integration, as illustrated in Figure 6-3. Each category has products suited to specific business needs. The reporting needs of an organization deal with routine reporting to visualize data in a more detailed format. Discovery and analysis requirements of an organization are met by delving deep into data and slicing and dicing it, which is done by analysts. Dashboards display KPIs and metrics in graphical interfaces.

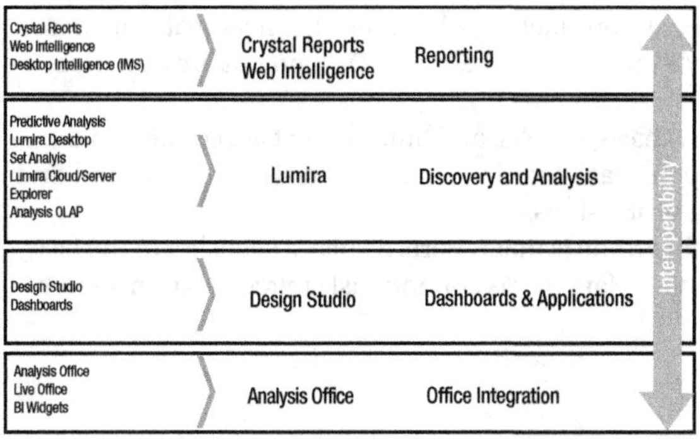

Figure 6-3. *The SAP Business Analytics product suite*

SAP Business Analytics products serve a great number of business requirements, from data discovery to mobile apps. Following is a list of business analytics tools, according to their function.

Reporting

This encompasses gathering and presenting data in a manner that makes it simple to understand the end consumer of the information. Reporting empowers end users with the knowledge to becoming expert in their area of business. The reporting tools provided by the SAP Business Analytics suite of products are

- SAP BusinessObjects Web Intelligence

- SAP Crystal Reports

- SAP BusinessObjects Explorer

Reports can be run by choosing certain time intervals or other filters. Reports are also delivered to business users' mailboxes in the form of PDFs or Excel files or to reporting platform inboxes.

Data Discovery and Analysis

SAP Lumira is the SAP process for data discovery, analysis, and visualization that features beautiful interactive graphs and infographics for impactful storytelling with data. SAP Lumira is fundamentally a self-service data visualization application for business users.

Owing to the columnar data storage mechanism used by Lumira, it retrieves data very quickly. A column-oriented database management system (DBMS) stores data tables as sections of columns of data, rather than as rows of data. Most relational databases store data in rows. As the column-based databases store only single columns of data, rather than entire rows, indexes are generally much smaller than the main table. By scanning smaller sets of data, the number of disk operations is reduced, thus making data retrieval faster.

Lumira has data-preparation features that are able to fetch data from Excel, SAP HANA, SQL, and SAP BW and blend it from these various sources. The data set can be further enriched by creating variables or hierarchies to enhance the data visualization and drill through it from the lowest level to the highest aggregation.

Dashboards and Applications

Design Studio and SAP Dashboards are the SAP dashboard products. Dashboards offer near real-time data visualization with capabilities to embed the dashboards into portals or e-mails. Dashboards are also mobile-compatible, making them available on tablets.

Dashboards contain various components, such as charts, graphs, and buttons, that are connected to data sources, to fetch data. The graphs and charts help the dashboard's consumers to visualize data and find trends and patterns, in order to make informed business decisions.

The main difference between reporting and dashboarding is that reports display a snapshot of the last refreshed data, whereas dashboards display near real-time data that is continuously refreshed from source systems through data connections.

Office Integrations

The BusinessObjects Live Office solution integrates seamlessly with Microsoft (MS) Office products. The huge advantage of integrating BusinessObjects Live Office into MS Office products is that data consumers do not have to learn new analytics tools. They can continue working with tools that they are used to, such as MS Excel or MS PowerPoint. Data from BusinessObjects Universes, Crystal Reports, and Web Intelligence can be fetched into Excel or PowerPoint via BusinessObjects Live Office.

Key Features of Each Product

Business Intelligence Platform

The Business Intelligence platform is one central platform from which to access many of the analytics products mentioned in the preceding section. As in Figure 6-2 and Figure 6-3, Web Intelligence, Crystal Reports, and analysis for OLAP (online analytical processing) and Lumira can be accessed from BI launch pad (see Figure 6-4).

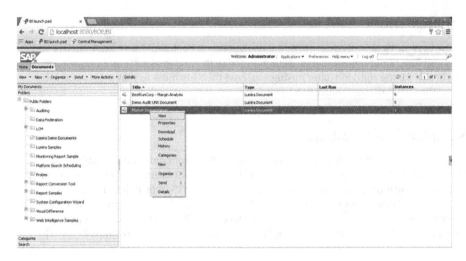

Figure 6-4. Accessing Lumira from within SAP BI launch pad

BI launch pad allows users to access various analytics tools with a single login and on a single platform, thereby making the BI launch pad user-friendly (see Figure 6-5). The other aspect of accessing the analytics tools on a single platform makes the data governance easier, as it is only a single platform that requires data access rules, rather than individual platforms.

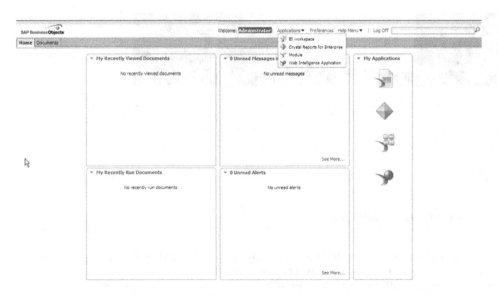

Figure 6-5. The SAP BI launch pad

The SAP BI platform shields business users from the complexities of data, providing them ready-to-use business intelligence data insights. The semantic layer between the data sources and the business layers handles the data transformations, making it easier for the business users. The semantic layers can manage a variety of data types and data sources from different database providers.

Business Analytics Tools

In this section, we delve into the details of each individual analytics tool. Each SAP Business Analytics tool serves some technical and functional requirements, as mentioned in the previous section. Organizations have to choose the right tool for the right job, after having analyzed their business requirements and the flexibilities provided by the SAP Business Analytics tools.

SAP BusinessObjects Design Studio

SAP BusinessObjects Design Studio allows designers to create applications for analysis and dashboards, based on SAP NetWeaver BW, SAP HANA, and BusinessObjects Universe data sources. Design Studio can be accessed as a stand-alone application as well, on the BI launch pad, SAP NetWeaver, or SAP HANA platform. Design Studio, apart from the obvious data-visualization functionalities, provides SDK support that enables it to access data from several sources. Figure 6-6 shows the home page of the SAP Design Studio designer, from which new applications can be created, recently used applications can be launched, and data sources added.

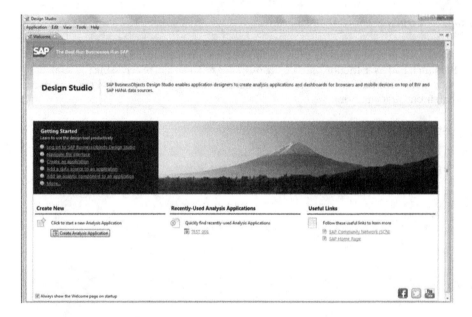

Figure 6-6. *Design Studio designer home page*

SAP Design Studio gives users the flexibility to create analysis applications based on SAP Netweaver, SAP HANA, and Universe, for browsers and mobile devices.

The main key features of SAP Design Studio are that it

- Offers full support for SAP NetWeaver BW and SAP HANA data models and engine capabilities

- Provides design tools to create applications, thereby eliminating the need for native HTML or iPad UI programming skills

- Can be used locally as well as embedded into the BI platform or integrated into SAP HANA and SAP NetWeaver

- Provides SDKs to further customize the default visualization features, thus allowing access to a broad range of data sources, such as web services and local files

Mobile Business Intelligence—SAP BusinessObjects Mobile App

This provides access to insights on the go for business users. SAP Mobile BI supports visualizations on SAP BusinessObjects, Web Intelligence, SAP Crystal Reports, SAP BusinessObjects Explorer, SAP Lumira, SAP Dashboards, and SAP Design Studio.

The SAP Mobile BI app can be customized to meet the specific needs of an organization. SAP Mobile BI has extensive features for smarter visualization capabilities, such as graphical cubes, customized maps, etc. SAP Mobile solutions are easy to deploy and distribute. Dashboards can be embedded into mobile apps, to make analytics a part of transactional apps. Employees are becoming more and more dependent on mobile devices, and some organizations also have a BYOD (bring your own device) policy, which makes it even more important to have a mobile BI strategy in place.

SAP Lumira

SAP Lumira is a fast, lightweight, in-memory server, platform, and portal. It facilitates quick deployment and sharing of information across departments, without much IT involvement. SAP Lumira can be downloaded, installed, configured, and prepared for usage very quickly. The installation process involves just a few clicks.

One of the key features of SAP Lumira is its ease of use and negligible learning curve. After having explored business data, discovered hidden insights, and created interactive visualizations, it is possible to share this content via the SAP Lumira Edge portal. The content resides in the SAP Lumira Edge document library and is available for easy viewing and interactive consumption via a web browser.

SAP Lumira can be purchased as a personal edition or in the standard edition, the personal edition being free for download. The personal edition allows data import from .xls and .csv files, but the standard edition allows data import from databases and SAP HANA apart from .xls and .csv files. Some other key features of SAP Lumira include the following:

- Easy to combine data from disparate sources in huge volumes

- Allows quick and easy ways to add calculations and groupings of data without any scripting or coding involved

- The data set analyzed in Lumira can be published to the SAP BI platform or exported to .xls or .csv files, to SAP Explorer (to be used as an information space), or to SAP HANA, as an analytic view.

- SAP Lumira can import data from a multitude of sources, such as .xls or .csv files and SAP HANA, or Apache Hadoop SAP BW, and freehand SQL query, to connect to a database.

- Data visualizations can be shared as stories, by combining graphics, text, and descriptions, linking to web sites or to another page in the story.

SAP Web Intelligence

This feature allows end-user flexibility, by providing trusted data from multiple sources.

The SAP Business Intelligence implementation is fairly simple and has a shorter time to market, making it very agile and lean. SAP Web Intelligence delivers new reports faster, meeting business requirements at an accelerated pace. Both the implementation and the development of new reports is fairly simple, thereby eliminating the need for many IT resources previously required.

SAP Crystal Reports

SAP Crystal Reports allows easy, affordable, self-serve information access to reports, dashboards, and search and exploration documents. SAP Crystal Server software delivers secure, personalized information sharing through a single semantic layer and server.

SAP Crystal Reports can connect to almost any data source—relational or OLAP, `.xls` files, and XML. Crystal Reports distribution within an organization can be managed independently with the Crystal server or embedded into business processes through office documents or portals, such as Microsoft Office and Microsoft SharePoint, or into applications, through SDKs (software developer kits).

Major advantages of Crystal Reports are

- Ease of use with a graphical interface

- Multisource data support

- Ability to create feature-rich pixel-perfect reports

- Ease of integrating Crystal reports into other applications, with SDKs

- That it is an enterprise reporting solution that can be made available via the Web or portals, making distribution to a large audience fairly simple.

SAP BusinessObjects Analysis

The SAP BusinessObjects Analysis edition for Microsoft Office is an Office add-in for multidimensional ad hoc analysis of OLAP sources in Excel. SAP BusinessObjects Analysis also allows BI presentations in PowerPoint. SAP BusinessObjects Analysis connects to SAP BEx queries, SAP NetWeaver BW, and SAP HANA.

SAP BusinessObjects Analysis provides the functionality that allows multiple cross tabs in a single Excel workbook with data from several sources, with easy-to-use drag-and-drop features.

SAP BusinessObjects Explorer

Business Explorer is a simple, intuitive tool to search for and drill down into data in BusinessObjects Universe, SAP HANA, or spreadsheets uploaded to the tool. Business Explorer can handle real-time data and does not require technical expertise, owing to its simplicity of use. Business Explorer can be accessed through the BI launch pad

Factors That Should Be Taken into Consideration While Choosing the Right Tool

As discussed, SAP provides a plethora of tools and services to serve the analytics requirements of an organization. Choosing the right tool for the right job, however, can be an overwhelming experience. Before selecting the right tool for the job at hand, organizations should evaluate their analytics needs against the tool, to determine the right fit.

- *Must-haves*: These are the key features that are absolutely necessary for meeting a business's analytics requirements, for example, the use of Hadoop to integrate big data. In the era of big data analytics, every customer interaction, every digital footprint, every tweet or Facebook share and like has become a vital source for generating business insights. To capture data that runs into petabytes, a big data solution such as Hadoop is required. SAP HANA allows integration with Hadoop, thus blending both structured data from points of sale, supply chains, ERP and CRM systems with unstructured data from social media.

- *Nice-to-haves*: The nice-to-have requirements could be defined as the ones that are not going to be used in the near future but could be an added value nevertheless. For example: being able to export reports into PDF format may not be a necessity, but it may be useful at some point of time, so it's good to know whether an analytics tool provides that feature.

- *Not-required*: Analytics tools can provide a lot of features that are not useful to an organization, thereby making them out of scope for evaluation. For example, a tool might provide integration possibilities with SAP NetWeaver, but the organization may not have plans ever to implement SAP NetWeaver.

Following are some key features of business analytics tools to consider when deciding whether or not a tool is the right one:

- Support for multiple data sources. In most organizations, there are multiple IT products, and it is a good analytics solution to have support for data integration with these sources.

- Data blending is a very important business requirement today, with more and more businesses analyzing the holistic view of a customer with data from multiple sources. It is important, therefore, to choose a BI tool that supports data blending from disparate sources.

- Web- and mobile-based interfaces are also important criteria to consider. Having a web-based interface eases the distribution of information among users, while mobile BI is becoming a predominant requirement for busy business users on the go.

- Visualization features with bars, graphs, pie charts, cross tabs and trend lines are a necessity for business users seeking to present data in an interactive way.

- Time to market is one of the most important factors to consider. If the time taken to implement a certain product is too long, it will not solve any near-term business requirements, which also could change by the time the product is fully rolled out.

- SDKs and plug-ins to embed business analytics tools into portals or other applications, such as SharePoint, should be considered.

- Data security is also one of the most important criteria to consider. A business analytics tool should be able to provide a means to restrict data access in a distributed environment. While most BI tools do provide data-access-granting mechanisms, the key is to find a tool that makes the process simple.

- The ability to export data to a PDF or Excel file or send it as mail attachments directly from the analytics tool are some other features to look for in a business analytics tool.

- Ease of upgrading the tools and the content in an easy manner is essential.

- Business analytics tools should provide the ability to create variables and formulae, drilling data into hierarchies, and easy report-customizing features.

- Scalability is an important aspect to consider for growing business needs. The amount of analytics content, the number of simultaneous users accessing the system, and the number of source systems that have to be integrated could increase exponentially, and a robust business analytics toll should be able to handle these changes.

- In-memory capability is also an important business requirement these days, owing to huge amounts of data having to be analyzed on the fly.

- Another important aspect to consider while choosing the right business analytics tool is learning curve. If a tool requires a huge amount of effort to learn on the part of users, then its adoption will be slow.

Consideration of all the preceding points while choosing the right tool serves as a guideline. There will, of course, be tools that match certain business requirements, but not all. But choosing a business analytics solution can mean a huge business investment; therefore, it is important to consider ROI (return on investment) before taking the plunge.

Implementation Case Study

Now that I have discussed the features of some of the main business analytics products offered by SAP and those to look for when choosing analytics products, let's consider a sample implementation.

Most organizations have several IT systems supporting the business processes that are their backbone. To understand which business processes or sales campaigns yield the most value, organizations have to measure the impact of business processes. Analytics is all about identifying and analyzing the factors that lead to the highs and lows of business performance, optimizing the processes further and measuring the impact of changes.

A media house that I worked for has many operations, apart from an online newspaper—online advertising, online health clubs, and classifieds. Each of these business areas has several KPIs, as illustrated in Figure 6-7.

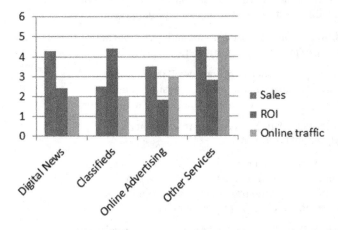

Figure 6-7. *Business areas of a media organization and key performance indicators for each area*

Each business area is defined separately, supported by different processes, and the KPIs are measured differently. For example, digital news sales are defined by the number of new customers acquired, whereas sales for online advertising could be both the number of customers that have paid to advertise their services, as well as the revenue generated from the number of clicks that each ad generates. The digital news is supported by various IT systems, such as

- Content management systems
- Web analytics systems to analyze the incoming traffic on the sites
- Sales systems that handle sales of new subscriptions
- CRM systems that handle customer data as well as marketing campaigns

- Invoicing systems that manage invoices sent to customers and accounting systems

- Ad servers that handle the ads displayed on the sites

Each of the preceding systems manages a specific type of function and so has data pertaining to that particular function. The data from the preceding systems are stored in some kind of database, and each system may allow simple reporting features to display metrics. But for analytics, the data from each business process has to be stored in a data warehouse, which then feeds reports and dashboards, as illustrated in Figure 6-8.

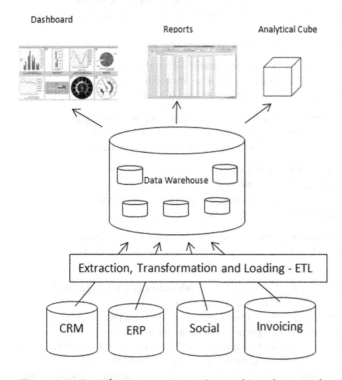

Figure 6-8. *Data from source systems is stored in a data warehouse that is a central data repository for enterprises*

The data from source systems can be fetched using SAP Data Services as explained in Chapter 4. Ad hoc reports are generated using SAP Web Intelligence, which is available to business users on the BI launch pad as well as via mail, as PDFs. SAP Lumira is used by the business controllers to analyze sales and marketing campaign data. SAP Design Studio is used to visualize the trends in sales and also the online traffic data, which provides near real-time data.

Business critical data resides in each of the source systems.

- CRM

- ERP

- Social Media

- Invoicing

- Content

- Image processing

- Contact center

- Ad servers

- Campaign systems

- Web analytics

Data in each system caters to one particular business process, and although some ERP or CRM systems provide reporting features, they are pretty basic and do not provide much insight about the business as a whole. Therefore, it is imperative to gather data from all the source systems that can add value to customer experience or improve business process efficiency.

While fetching data from each of these sources, a few points have to be kept in mind.

- Check the means for data integration. Can flat files be extracted from the source systems directly and fed into the ETL flows, or should they be fetched from FTP (file transfer protocol) servers, in which case FTP servers would have to be set up.

- While building the ETL flows, the work flows have to contain business rules and logic that the business has to define. As rules often change in today's dynamic business scene, the ETL work flows must be agile enough to adapt to these changes quickly.

- Business logic often resides in ETL work flows, but some business analytics visualizations may require that some of the logic be built into reports. In such cases, it must be clearly defined which business rules reside in the data warehouse and the ETL work flows and which business rules are to be built in the reporting layer.

- The data in the data warehouse should be granular enough both to facilitate drilling and slicing and dicing of data in the reporting layers and also create calculated fields, according to need.

Other business domains, such as online advertising, classifieds, and other services, are supported by several business processes that cater to specific business areas and processes.

The challenge, however, is maintaining an increasing number of reporting and dashboard requirements, growing numbers of users, and the increasing amount of data. In order to resolve these issue with increasing business data visualization needs, SAP Lumira and SAP Business Intelligence Live Office user licenses can be increased, enabling the business users to analyze data themselves, with little IT involvement. This is, of course, an uphill task, initially, but with adequate amount of training and knowledge sharing, business can manage some of their data analysis needs by themselves.

The challenges faced by an analytics team are constantly changing. They could involve handling a large number of reporting requirements, managing the different data access levels required for adequate data security, or adding more data source systems to pump data into the enterprise data warehouse.

With the advance of SAP Business Analytics offerings and integration feasibilities with newer data sources, data analysis using SAP Business Analytics is the right choice for enterprises.

Following are some of the usual reporting needs of a business:

- *Operational reporting*: Reports pertaining to the operational status of systems

- *Performance reporting*: Reports that provide insights regarding performance of products, sales, or campaigns

- *Data validation reporting*: Reports that provide information regarding data quality

- *Data reconciliation reporting*: Reports such as these provide insights into data synchronization in the source system and the target systems. Even if there could be business rules applied, the data in the data warehouse and the reports and dashboards should still match the data in the source systems.

- *KPIs*: Last but not the least are the KPIs (key performance indicators). KPIs give a clear picture of the business drivers at a glance. KPIs at a very high level could be the total customer base or the total number of products sold—weekly, monthly, or by year-on-year growth, etc.

Figure 6-9 displays the flow of data for a business analytics practice at the enterprise level.

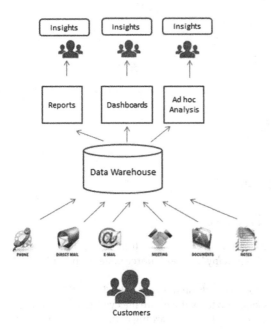

Figure 6-9. *Business analytics practice in day-to-day business*

A customer-centric approach to doing business starts with gathering as much data as possible about customers, from customer registration forms. When a customer approaches the point of sale, and salespeople enter the customer details in an ERP system, the data becomes available for analytics by means of ETL flows from the ERP database to the data warehouse. The customer data can then be further refined, by adding market research data about customer purchase behavior and also data from the customer interaction with the contact center or through invoicing and e-mails sent and responded to.

Refining a customer database is an ongoing process that will require much time and effort to keep updated. Once data from all customer interactions across all channels is stored in a data warehouse, which could be Oracle, SQL Server, or SAP HANA, the same can be visualized using SAP Business Analytics products, as described previously, per the business requirements. For example, using SAP Dashboards for KPIs, SAP Web Intelligence for static reporting, or SAP Lumira for analysis.

Once the data is visualized by business analysts, business controllers, and C-level executives in reports and dashboards, insights that can be used to further improve business processes and optimize products are generated. The response data from the optimized systems is again fed back into the data warehouse, to analyze the results of optimization.

Figure 6-10 shows the different kinds of data generated at different stages of business processes in an organization. The data generated at each stage should be stored for further analysis, to gain insights. The SAP Business Analytics suite of products can help analyze the data at each stage of the business processes.

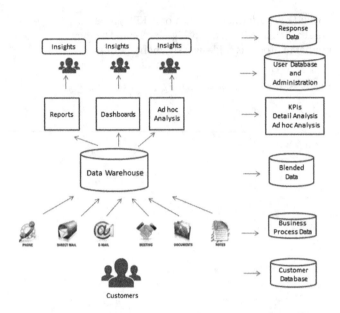

Figure 6-10. *The data points that are aligned with business analytics*

Using SAP Lumira, SAP Web Intelligence, or SAP Dashboards to visualize data from the customer base, or the data in the data warehouse that contains data from many business source systems, provides an understanding of key business drivers.

The way data is centered or structured in an organization depends on the kind of business. If it is a product company that sells products or services, it is as essential to track the entire life cycle of products as it is to track information regarding customers. As shown in Figure 6-11, data regarding a product development life cycle is stored. As well, data about a customer's interaction with a product, spread across several channels, is also stored.

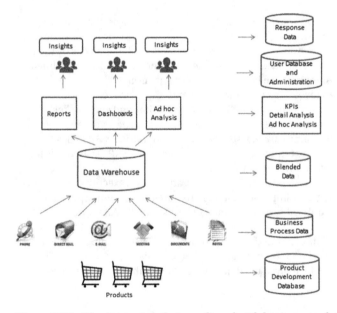

Figure 6-11. *The data points that are aligned with business analytics from a product-development perspective*

The insights that are gained after the business analysts, business controllers, and product analysts have analyzed the data are used to enhance product features and further improve customer experience with the products.

Analytics is defining the way organizations conduct business, the way marketing and sales teams market products and services, the way products are developed, and the way organizations perform competitive analysis. Data from every single business process should be gathered and stored, to conduct trend analysis and performance reporting, not only to better understand the business processes, but also to tweak them to increase customer satisfaction.

Data from all touch points that the customer uses to interact with businesses should also be gathered, to understand customer behavior and to be proactive, rather than reactive, in pleasing the customer.

Figure 6-12 sums up the business analytics implementation goals, purpose, and methodology at a very high level.

Figure 6-12. *Business analytics functions*

Business analytics is concerned with gathering and analyzing data at every stage of business processes, to measure and optimize products, processes, and services. SAP Business Analytics products can help organizations bridge the gap between business and IT, by helping organizations visualize their data, thus improving understanding of their

- Customer base

- Product offerings and reception

- Marketing efforts

- UX design

- Web behavior

- App behavior

- Sales figures

- Inventory, etc.

CHAPTER 7

■ ■ ■

SAP Analytics Product Implementation

In this chapter, you will learn some practical technical implementations of SAP Business Analytics and some industry standards related to business analytics projects.

Overview of SAP Analytics Product Capabilities for Some Mainstream Industries

As I have discussed, all businesses are supported by a number of IT systems and products that automatize the business process, reducing manual intervention. When most of the processes are automated, business- and IT people are able to use their time more efficiently, for innovative purposes within their scope of business activity.

As in Figure 7-1, the need for business analytics arises from the fact that businesses have to understand their own organizational processes better, to better serve their end customers.

Figure 7-1. *The factors driving business analytics*

For organizations, this results in a continuous process to analyze, understand, conduct tests, and evaluate results, in order to facilitate

- Better business insights

- Brand awareness

- Revenue generation

- Customer experience

- Customer loyalty

The most common business areas that require IT support are

- Customer Relationship Management (CRM)

- Enterprise Resource Planning (ERP)

- Product Life Cycle Management (PLM)

- Supply Chain Management (SCM)

- Supplier Relationship Management (SRM)

With a lot of focus placed on attracting more traffic to web sites and mobile apps, there is a great deal of emphasis on web and mobile analytics recently. Data from all the aforementioned business areas has to be integrated into a common platform, to provide a holistic view of a business.

SAP provides industry-specific solutions, such as the following:

- SAP for Retail (ISR)

- SAP for Utilities (ISU)

- SAP for Public Sector (IS PSCD)

- SAP for Oil & Gas (IS Oil & Gas)

- SAP for Telecommunications (IST)

- SAP for Healthcare (ISH)

- SAP for Banking (SAP for Banking)

- SAP for Insurance (SAP for Insurance)

- SAP Financial Services Network (FSN)

- SAP Shipping Services Network (SSN)

- Engineering Construction & Operations (EC&O)

Some solutions do come with reporting features, but in order to use advance analytics and data mining, SAP Business Analytics products have to be used to gain in-depth insights about business data. As in Figure 7-2, business data resides in IT systems that support businesses, namely, ERP, CRM, etc., which are then blended using data integration, which fetches data from each of the systems and saves it in a data warehouse. The data warehouse then feeds the reports, dashboards, ad hoc analysis, and data mining.

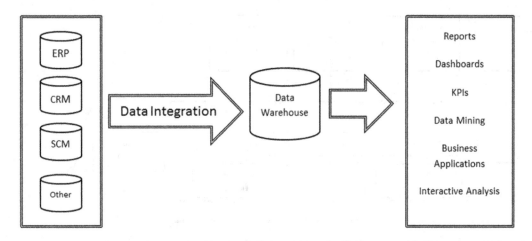

Figure 7-2. *Fundamental principles of business analytics, irrespective of the industry*

SAP provides a number of solutions in the SAP Business Analytics suite of products, such as

- SAP BusinessObjects Analysis
- SAP BusinessObjects Business Intelligence
- SAP BusinessObjects Dashboards
- SAP BusinessObjects Design Studio
- SAP BusinessObjects Explorer
- SAP Cloud for Analytics
- SAP Crystal Reports
- SAP Crystal Server
- SAP Lumira
- SAP Predictive Analytics

As shown in Figure 7-3, SAP has a wide range of advanced analytics offerings. SAP HANA, which is SAP's in-memory database for advanced data processing and flexible data integration services, is a database for real-time analytics, with faster data retrieval abilities. Using SAP HANA as the underlying layer for data storage and retrieval gives big enterprise companies a competitive edge as far as real-time analytics is concerned. SAP Data Services enables the data transfer between different solutions and platforms. SAP Business Analytics has a whole suite of products that help business users with different needs gain access to the information required in a very simple and efficient manner. SAP Business Analytics also supports many partner business intelligence (BI) tools and applications.

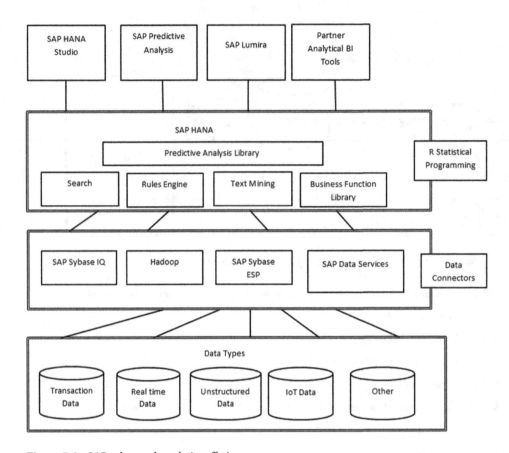

Figure 7-3. *SAP advanced analytics offerings*

Data sources can be very different, depending on the industry in question, and can include real-time data, unstructured data from social media, IoT (Internet of things) data from sensors and wearables, or transactional data from business systems. Some of the source systems could be SAP-based products, allowing easier integration to SAP HANA or SAP Sybase. Non-SAP products can be integrated with SAP HANA, using SAP Data Services as the ETL (extraction, transformation, and loading) tool. Data can be analyzed further in SAP Lumira or used for data mining, by using SAP Predictive Analytics.

Examples of Some SAP Analytics Implementations

Having worked extensively with BI implementations, I have come across a number of successful BI programs and projects. The single most important criteria that determines the success of a BI project is getting the business requirements right by asking the right questions. It is also important to have a business sponsor as part of the business analytics project, to drive the business case. Typically, a business analytics project consists of the following team members:

- A business sponsor, to create a business case for investment and follow up on the business value being generated in a project

- A technical architect, who is well versed not only with industry knowledge but also able to translate business requirements into technical solution architecture

- Business analysts, to analyze the business requirements and business processes that influence the technical design and architecture

- Business analytics developers, who implement the technical architecture by developing data flows from source systems to a common data warehouse and develop reports and dashboards

- Data analysts, who conduct sanity checks to identify data-quality issues. A data analyst might also check that the technical implementation of business rules lead to correct results.

Figure 7-4 illustrates customer journey mapping, which is a necessary step to identify all the processes that a customer has to undertake to avail himself/herself of the products or services a company offers. A similar mapping journey can be done to understand the product life cycle and points that are in need of reassessment, optimization, and new implementations.

Figure 7-4. *Customer journey mapping*

The fine lines between different IT systems is getting blurred as data becomes paramount. To gain insights, data from several systems must be merged, providing a holistic view.

A business analytics project should have certain encapsulated features, to qualify as a well-implemented project. As listed in Figure 7-5, the key steps in a business analytics implementation project have to be defined at the inception of a project.

1. Customer journey mapping
2. Identify business processes at each customer touch point
3. Identify supporting IT systems for each business process
4. Identify the dependencies for each business process and IT system
5. Define the future data strategy
6. Define the data strategy implementation
7. As-is to-be gap analysis
8. Feasibility study
9. Design the solution architecture for to-be
10. Design the tech architecture for to-be
11. Risk analysis
12. Identify the skillsets required
13. Budget, time line, and resourcing
14. Begin with small iterations and then scale

Figure 7-5. *A typical business analytics roadmap*

The key steps are

1. Mapping a customer or product journey over the entire life cycle

2. Once the life cycle is plotted, it is easier to identify the business processes that are involved at each step of the journey.

3. Once the business processes are identified, it is not very difficult to understand the IT systems that support each business process and the integrations that are in place.

4. Next comes the need to state the to-be data strategy, depending on the business goals of the organization.

5. Once the future goals are defined, it is necessary to take stock of the current data structures and systems, to understand the parts that can continue to function and the ones that have to be renewed.

6. A gap analysis has to be done, to understand the new requirements for the business processes and the IT systems.

7. A solution design and IT architecture has to be designed, to deliver the future data strategy.

8. The next step is to identify the skillsets required to deliver such a solution, both functionally and technically.

9. Once the implementation life cycle begins, it is vital to build and test in small iterations, to analyze the cause and effect of new implementations.

While it is important to bear in mind the steps that lead to a successful implementation of a business analytics project or program, it is also important to understand what the key features that define a successful business analytics implementation program are. Some of the key features that a robust business analytics project embodies are as follows:

- Fulfills the business requirements and can adapt easily to newer business needs

- Adds value in the form of process optimization or cost reduction or generates value for the end customer

- Has a short time to market, reducing the implementation time and yielding value very quickly in the process

- Is flexible enough so that it is easy to refactor or integrate new sources of data

- Carries low maintenance costs. A solution that requires very detailed supervision and is not fault tolerant is not an optimum solution.

Owing to the Internet, the amount of data produced by businesses has been growing constantly. Every industry wants to monetize data, to initiate data-driven decisions that expedite revenue generation, enhance customer experience, and drive innovation. Analyzing customer data generates information about customer preferences and behavior, which, in turn, leads to new market opportunities for some businesses. Many organizations have merged or acquired companies that provide services ancillary to their own, in order to serve their customers better by providing a complete package of services.

Figure 7-6 illustrates the different phases of an analytics project. In order to implement a business analytics project, the first step is to ensure that the business analytics program office decides the purpose(s) and goals of implementing a business analytics project and obtains a fair understanding of the high-level requirements. In the planning phase, the analytics program office has to gather both the high- and low-level requirements—the milestones of the project—and define and put in place the technical team. In the design phase, the technical team designs the architecture, the data flow from end to end, and the reporting and dashboarding layouts. The actual implementation of the design takes place in the build phase, in which the ETL and the reports are developed, systems are tested, including by the end user during user acceptance testing. If the end users are satisfied with the outcomes, the analytics solution is implemented in production, and thereafter handed over to a maintenance team for routine maintenance, upgrading, fixes, and enhancements to the solution.

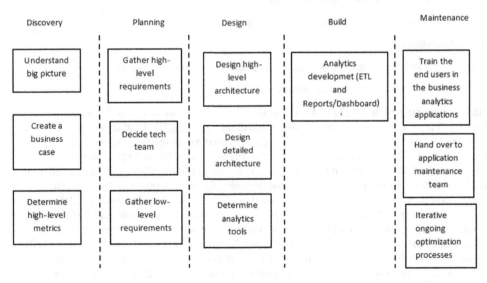

Figure 7-6. *The different phases in a business analytics project*

The implementation cycle, however, is not free of hassles. Requirements change midway, which may result in efforts getting wasted or a delay in deadlines, due to new requirements that necessitate new design and build efforts. Thus, it is important to maintain some project artifacts, as an issue log and change log, to document the issues that come up during any phase of the project and the solution implemented. The change log documents all the changes that have occurred during the implementation cycle of a project that have resulted in deviations. These artifacts are separate from budget and resource-planning documents.

As mentioned, the different phases of an analytics project are shown in Figure 7-6. In the first phase of the project, high-level goals must be determined. In other words, an organization has to be clear about its goals in regard to implementing an analytics project and about what the expectations are from the implementation. Analytics projects are put into practice to transform quantitative capabilities into purposeful and impactful decision making. In order to quantify business goals, KPIs (key performance indicators) that effectively measure business goals have to be determined.

Railway Company Example

One practical example of business analytics are railway companies, which place a lot of emphasis on punctuality, onboard experience, and customer service. Let's consider a hypothetical railway company called ABC that has a huge fleet of trains operating between different destinations, sells journeys directly to customers (online and via franchisee units), and also serves food and beverages onboard. So, ABC has a lot of different services to cater to, potentially making the IT architecture quite complex. There are different kinds of insights that can be generated from the business, depending on the need.

Some of the main KPIs in such a railway company could be

- Punctuality of the trains

- Canceled train services

- Number of trains in transit in real time

- Sales revenue from ticket sales

- Sales revenue from ticket sales online

- Sales revenue from ticket sales via franchisees

- Sales revenue from onboard sales

- Peak season sales

- Social media metrics, such as Facebook likes, comments, shares, and tweets

- Trend analysis, to check the trends of sales

In order to hone in on the preceding KPIs, a number of systems are involved, e.g., ticket booking systems, systems that maintain train timetables, systems that maintain actual information about trains running at the moment, financial accounting systems, and social media management systems, apart from the data warehouse that maintains historic data about the journeys, passengers, and sales figures.

Because the amount of data is quite huge, the data retrieval time could be substantial, so to avoid that, SAP HANA will be used as the in-memory column-based database. SAP HANA provides the infrastructure and tools for building high-performance applications, based on the SAP HANA engine, which is data-source agonistic. SAP Data Services is being used as the ETL tool for extraction, transformation, and loading of data from different source systems into SAP BW Enterprise Data Warehouse, which enables the data to be pre-computed, making data retrieval faster in SAP BusinessObjects Web Intelligence and SAP Analysis for Office. As far as dashboards used to display the train punctuality KPIs are concerned—trains in transit, number of trains undergoing maintenance work, etc.—SAP Design Studio will be used. SAP Design Studio provides full and native support of BW BEx queries, direct connectivity to HANA, as well as an advanced scripting engine, and is suited to mobile devices. Data distribution is also fairly simple and can be managed from SAP BI launch pad, which makes the experience seamless for the users of different business analytics platforms. SAP Lumira is used as a self-service BI application by business users, to conduct data analysis. All this is shown in Figure 7-7.

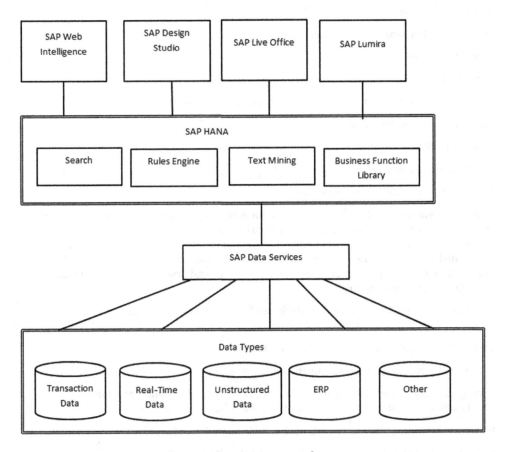

Figure 7-7. *SAP Business Analytics implementation example*

Self-service BI by means of SAP Lumira requires some initial technical training on the part of end users in the finance team. But once the non-IT business controllers get numbers crunching, using a business analytics product, the IT team will be left to implement new business requirements.

Media Company Example

Another real-life example of SAP Business Analytics implementation is a media company that has state-of-the-art infrastructure to analyze web traffic data, behavioral analytics, sales and marketing, CRM campaigns, and online advertising.

Media outlets are no longer traditional print media distribution companies. With advanced technology, media companies have to be on their toes, producing content that not only attracts subscribers but also creates online platforms on which big brands are able to advertise their products and services. The main KPIs that drive the different business areas of a media company are broadly stated as follows:

- Number of visitors to the site

- Number of downloads of the app

- Number of visitors per channel (mobile, web)

- Number of online advertisements booked

- Number of online advertisements per industry segment

- Number campaigns sent out

- Number of campaigns that lead to consumers taking action

- Number of campaigns that lead to consumers deregistering the e-mails or SMS

- Number of subscriptions sold

- Most read articles

- Most followed authors

- Highest revenue-generating customers

The preceding lists only a few of the KPIs that media companies calculate, but there are a number of trend analyses that media outlets have to perform to gain insights about their customer base and the needs of potential customers. By analyzing the traffic on web sites, content can be adjusted to attract even more traffic, in real time. Media companies also segment and classify their customer base, to better provide quality content that is aptly targeted to their audience. A few of the IT systems and products that support media companies and their related businesses are

- CMS (content management systems), which handle the content on web sites for publishing from a central interface

- Web analytics tools, to analyze the traffic on sites

- CRM systems, to manage customer interactions

- Campaign management systems, to handle campaigns sent to customers as e-mails, weekly newsletters, or push notifications on the site or in the mobile app

- Financial accounting systems, to keep track of finances and bookkeeping

- Order booking systems, to manage sales orders booked by the sales team

- Ad servers, which handle displaying of ads on the web sites and the mobile apps

- Integration platforms, which integrate data from different sources

- Invoicing systems

- Data warehouses, which store historic data regarding customer information, financial information, invoicing history, ad server details, and distribution details

Data from each of these systems is fetched using SAP Data Services as the ETL tool and placed into a database, which is an Oracle database but could also be SAP HANA, owing to HANA's fast performance of queries and analytics on very large amounts of data. The first layer of integration is a one-to-one mapping from the source systems, but in the subsequent layers, the data is cleansed and modified using business rules and then stored in the data warehouse, which handles version controlling of historical data and feeds the several reports and dashboards. Version controlling of data means handling the changes in customer or product history that are relevant from a business perspective.

Once data from source systems is analyzed and insights are gained, the processes are optimized, using the feedback. Once the processes are optimized, the new response data can be used for further analysis and to gain even newer insights, creating a feedback loop. This kind of experimentation leads to continuous improvement of business processes and effectiveness.

Once the source data is stored in the data warehouse, the data can be displayed in static reports, using SAP Business Objects Web Intelligence or SAP Dashboards. Data can be used for early stage data discovery, using SAP Lumira. SAP Predictive Analytics can be used for advanced data exploration. SAP BI launch pad is the central interface used for access rights and administration of users and groups for different SAP Business Analytics tools. Depending on the comfort level of users, SAP Business Analytics can be tailored to suit the specific business needs.

The rules of thumb for any business analytics project are basically the same. As business systems now also include data from social media platforms, data from apps, and ratings that customers give to products and services, they hold a lot of additional information about customers. Consumer information is no longer exclusively about data from structured transactional systems that has to be stored and analyzed in order to gain a holistic view of customers and the main business drivers. Now, every data source that leads to an insight about a business should be included in an analytics project.

The business analytics team members have an important role to play in the implementation life cycle, and not just technically. Analytics team members have to understand the entire business process, the factors that lead to revenue generation, the marketing campaign targets, the targeted audience, and the potential customer base, as well as customer behavior. Some companies also do competitive analysis and analyze market research data to better understand the market before even trying to increase their market share.

Upcoming Trends in Business Analytics

With the ever-increasing amount of data and with data being used to drive businesses, data and the insights it provides will become even more important in the near future. Companies are getting more tech-oriented, in order to reach out and retain customers, using innovative means. The focus is shifting from products that companies sell to the customers that are or will be users of these products. Companies will have to proactively find means of attracting customers to ensure their loyalty. Because customers today are very demanding, it becomes even more important to use data to find the right audience to market products and services to. Once customers are acquired, it is important to analyze every aspect of their consumer experience, to be able to serve them better and personalize targeted campaigns more efficiently.

Some key trends in the business analytics field that seem to be emerging and will likely continue for a while are

- *Data visualization*: This becomes paramount for displaying in a simple manner for business users key performance indicators that drive businesses. Data is being used to narrate stories about customers and products in brand-building efforts. Data visualization makes it easier for both technical and nontechnical users to understand data.

- *Mobile business analytics*: As the number of devices grows, business analytics on mobile is becoming more and more advanced. Mobile business analytics is branching out as a platform of its own, rather than as a rudimentary feature of business analytics. Mobile solutions are being developed in a way that makes consumers' experience seamless when switching between devices.

- *IoT*: In a connected world of smart homes and wearables, business analytics makes sense of all the data from multiple sources used to derive insights into process optimization and product development.

- *Social media management*: The way we converse and socialize has changed a lot in the past few years. From finding friends to checking reviews about products to booking tickets and finding jobs, most day-to-day activities have an online touchpoint at some junction. Business analytics will have to develop APIs and integration methods to connect to the social media platforms, to analyze the huge amount of unstructured data being generated.

- *Cloud analytics*: As the amount of data generated increases, so does the complexity of storing it. But with the advent of cloud computing, scalability has become easier, along with infrastructure maintenance. Business analytics solutions are introducing a number of connectors to different types of data sources, cloud sources being one of the most important.

- *Data integration*: The importance of data blending has been rising as a 360-degree view of customer or business life cycles has become paramount. But in order to blend data from different sources, data integration is required, which, in turn, requires that a business analytics tool provide data connectors to many sources. Data integration has to be a simpler process than it is today, to promote the democratization of data from disparate sources and make it available to a wider audience, without hassles.

- *Self-service BI*: As data is the buzzword that has engulfed every single business area, business users depend a lot more on data for decision making. It is thus imperative to empower business users, who may not be very tech-savvy. So, easy-to-use business analytics tools are the demand of the day. More and more business analytics tools are providing self-service business analytics, so that business users do not have to depend on IT intervention for minor requirements.

As the analytics field gets more and more advanced, the line between marketing, web analytics, CRM, IoT, wearables, gaming, etc., becomes blurred. Omni channel data from every touchpoint contributes to insights about customer behavior. Business analytics is the art of combining data from disparate sources and making this information available in a way that is simple, easy, and fast, while generating value for business drivers.

Figure 7-8 shows the way the business analytics products, platforms, and functionalities are evolving. There is a lot of thrust on predictive analytics, more pixel-perfect visualizations, and traditional BI. The thrust, however is more on speed of delivery, in real time. Hence, it becomes very important to choose the right hardware, as well as software platforms, to deliver a complete package of solutions to business needs. Big data is defined by the three V's:

- Variety

- Velocity

- Volume

The right business analytics should be able to deliver, taking into account the aforementioned three factors of variety, velocity, and volume.

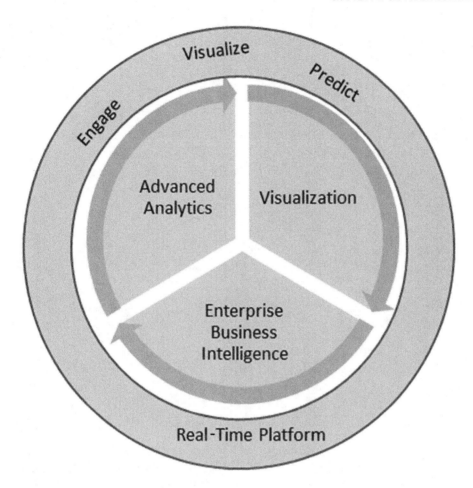

Figure 7-8. *Business analytics platform evolution*

With the popularity of columnar databases rising, insights can be gained almost in real time. This in itself is a huge leap for the business analytics field. Data can be visualized in real time to analyze the pros and cons and causes and effects of different variations in data. This can lead to huge business gains.

There are ample reasons for organizations to implement business analytics at the enterprise level. It is a matter of choosing the right implementation technique, processes, team, and tools.

Index

A

ABAP Data Services versions 4.2, 28
Application Programming Interface (APIs), 4

B

Bill Inmon architecture, 39
Business intelligence (BI) programs
    build phase, 93
    business analytics project, 90–91, 93
    customer journey mapping, 91
    different phases, 93
    the Internet, 93
    planning phase, 93
    typical business analytics roadmap, 92
Business analytics
    applications, 2
    challenges, 4–5
    cloud analytics, 98
    columnar databases, 99
    data integration, 98
    data visualization, 97
    developers, 5
    evolution, 99
    factors, 98
    implications, 2–4
    information, 1
    IoT, 97
    market analysis data, 1
    mobile business analytics, 97
    online, 2
    pixel-perfect visualizations, 98
    process, 1–2
    self-service BI, 98
    social media management, 98

C

Call detail record (CDR), 52
Central Management Console (CMC), 28
Central repositories, 32
Combine data sources
    blending data, 25
    data cleansing, 22
    data silos, 23
    data warehouse, 22
    integrated business rules, 23
    master data management systems, 23
    removing duplicates, 23
    SAP business analytics, 24–25
Content management system (CMS) data, 3

D

Data cleansing, 22
Data integration scenario
    business needs, 18–19
    data formats, 20–21
    data governance issues, 19
    data-quality issues, 19
    ETL process, 18
    historical records, 20
    sources, 18
    techniques, 21
Data silos, 16
DimSalesPerson points, 36

E, F, G

Enterprise Resource Planning (ERP) system, 17
Extraction, transformation and loading (ETL), 4, 18,
    27–28, 32, 34–35, 38, 41–46, 48–54

© Sudipa DuttaRoy 2016
S. DuttaRoy, *SAP Business Analytics*, DOI 10.1007/978-1-4842-1383-4

■ U, V, W, X, Y, Z

Get the eBook for only $4.99!

Why limit yourself?

Now you can take the weightless companion with you wherever you go and access your content on your PC, phone, tablet, or reader.

Since you've purchased this print book, we are happy to offer you the eBook for just $4.99.

Convenient and fully searchable, the PDF version enables you to easily find and copy code—or perform examples by quickly toggling between instructions and applications.

To learn more, go to http://www.apress.com/us/shop/companion or contact support@apress.com.

Printed in the United States
By Bookmasters